CATHEDRALS OF BRITAIN

David Pepin

Published in Great Britain in 2016 by Shire Publications Ltd (part of Bloomsbury Publishing Plc), PO Box 883, Oxford, OX1 9PL, UK.

PO Box 3985, New York, NY 10185-3985, USA.

E-mail: shire@shirebooks.co.uk www.shirebooks.co.uk

First published as *Discovering Cathedrals*, no. 112 in the Shire 'Discovering' series, in 1971, 1994 and 2004. This new book comprises an extensively revised image selection and entirely new design.

A CIP catalogue record for this book is available from the British Library.

Shire Library no. 831. ISBN-13: 978 1 78442 049 9

PDF e-book ISBN: 9781784421045

ePub ISBN: 9781784421038

David Pepin has asserted his right under the Copyright, Designs and Patents Act, 1988, to be identified as the author of this book.

Typeset in Garamond Pro and Gill Sans.

Printed in China through World Print Ltd.

16 17 18 19 20   10 9 8 7 6 5 4 3 2 1

COVER IMAGE
Front cover: the octagonal crossing tower at Ely Cathedral. Back cover: The famous twelfth-century knocker on the north door at Durham Cathedral.

TITLE PAGE IMAGE
Worcester Cathedral beautifully illuminated by night.

CONTENTS PAGE IMAGE
Assembling for the Easter Procession at Wells Cathedral, which celebrates the Resurrection of Jesus Christ, and is the most important festival of the Christian year.

DEDICATION
For June, Nick and Tom.

AUTHOR'S NOTE
Every effort has been made to provide correct information in the section on individual cathedrals, but from time to time movable objects, furnishings, monuments and such like may be changed or relocated. Furthermore new works of art constantly enhance the glory of our cathedral churches. Although this book is about rare things and beautiful buildings the author stresses that people come first and that when marvelling at the architecture one should not lose sight of the buildings' ecumenical purpose and function in the community. A stroll around can become a purposeful 'spiritual' journey or pilgrimage, an experience to enrich long after leaving the building, which radiates stability, continuity and timelessness.

Shire Publications is supporting the Woodland Trust, the UK's leading woodland conservation charity, by funding the dedication of trees.

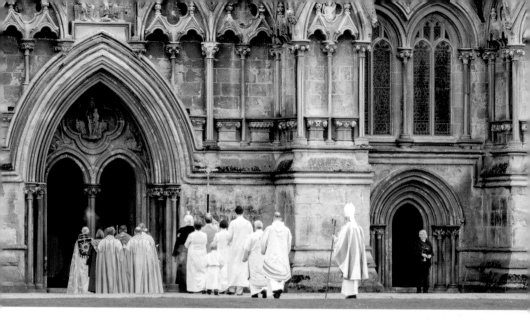

CONTENTS

ANGLICAN CATHEDRALS OF ENGLAND AND WALES

ROMAN CATHOLIC CATHEDRALS OF ENGLAND AND WALES

CATHEDRALS OF SCOTLAND

INTRODUCTION

CERTAIN OF BRITAIN'S cathedrals rank as architectural landmarks of the highest order, even when they are compared with their counterparts in the rest of Europe. Each cathedral is unique and even the modest ones, whose architecture is less attractive, often possess features and treasures which are unknown elsewhere.

Many people who visit these national shrines – and year by year more and more are joining their ranks – will naturally have their favourites.

Cathedrals are not museums. While they embody much of great beauty and historical interest, first and foremost they are places of worship and, ideally, centres of service, connected with people past and present. The beauty associated with the worship conveyed in the music, ceremonial and architecture stems from a great faith through the ages. Of course it is not wrong simply to enjoy the architecture, but to know why a church or cathedral was built in the first place adds to this enjoyment. To inspire us there is the architectural beauty of the 'sacred space', the worship and music. Even in the silence, in the peace and quiet, something of the 'divine come down to earth' will hopefully be experienced, and

Ely Cathedral: an East Anglian medieval masterpiece, photographed unusually in winter. From afar, across the Fens, the cathedral appears like a ship on an ocean, an unforgettable sight.

also the relevance of our nation's diverse Christian heritage.

The building, therefore, is an expression of something deeper than the mere bricks and stones themselves. A cathedral is not an end in itself. Without people a cathedral is an empty shell. It is the faithful residents who worship in the place regularly, the many people who maintain the building in a host of ways and the casual worshippers and visitors, all these, who are the life of the cathedral and its *raison d'être*. Each cathedral has a distinct atmosphere, a personality. It is hoped that the following historical and architectural notes will enable readers to get to know these personalities and through their own experience 'discover' the cathedrals for themselves.

Chichester: Sir George Gilbert Scott's spire and tower of 1886 replaced the Norman tower and early fifteenth-century spire which collapsed in 1861.

A cathedral usually has an organisation known as 'The Friends' who have the welfare of the cathedral at heart and will always welcome other like-minded people as members. The Ministry of Welcome, visitors' centres, cathedral camps for students, education centres and permanent exhibitions interpreting the work of the cathedral are also becoming familiar features of cathedral life and all providing a vital service to the local and wider community. The author is grateful to many people, both clergy and lay, who have willingly helped in his pursuit of exploring and discovering. He also thanks the staff at Shire Publications and especially Jacqueline Fearn, Elizabeth Crawford and Russell Butcher for their assistance and forbearance.

Alston, Cumbria, 2015.

WHAT IS A CATHEDRAL?

A CATHEDRAL IS the main church in a church district known as a diocese (in this case Anglican or Church of England) where the bishop of the diocese has his cathedra or throne. 'Cathedra' means chair, hence the word cathedral for the special church. Usually the largest church in an area fulfils this function, with all that this entails in the way of special services, concerts, diocesan and children's festivals and popular events like pilgrimages. There is also the daily round of worship even when very few people are present, but nonetheless on behalf of the whole diocese. There are a few very small cathedrals, however, and also some very large abbeys of cathedral-like proportions, such as Westminster, Bath and Tewkesbury, which are not cathedrals. It is the bishop's cathedra alone that gives a church cathedral status.

Cathedrals are in an ideal position to foster cultural and pastoral exchange and many links are being forged with cathedrals and dioceses in other parts of the world. Ecumenical chaplains and links with other Faith communities are also part of a cathedral's life and influence. At present there are forty-six dioceses (but forty-eight Anglican cathedrals) in England and Wales, plus Peel, Isle of Man. Each diocese is made up of many parishes, grouped also in deaneries.

Everyone in Britain has a parish church and a cathedral. In England there are two provinces, Canterbury and York. The former includes those dioceses south of a line running

St Augustine's Chair, Canterbury Cathedral. Every Archbishop of Canterbury is enthroned in this ancient and very special seat or 'cathedra'. A cathedral is a church in which there is the official 'chair' (cathedra or throne) of the bishop of that diocese. Every cathedral church must have one.

Pilgrims of all ages gather at St Albans. This is one of the ancient abbeys that, after the dissolution of the monasteries 500 years ago, had a new lease of life, first as a parish church (which it still is) and then, from 1877, as the cathedral church for Bedfordshire and Hertsfordshire.

from north Shropshire, Staffordshire, east Derbyshire, Leicestershire and Lincolnshire to the Humber. The dioceses north of the line constitute the York province, of which three have been amalgamated (Bradford, Ripon/Leeds and Wakefield) – together known as the Diocese of West Yorkshire and the Dales. Both provinces have their own archbishop; the Archbishop of York is styled Primate of England, while the Archbishop of Canterbury is Primate of *All* England. The Church in Wales covers six dioceses and has its own archbishop. Only the Archbishops of Canterbury and York and the Bishops of London, Durham and Winchester have permanent seats in the House of Lords. Twenty-one of the remaining bishops sit in the upper house according to their dates of seniority as bishops.

A cathedral is run by a special staff called a chapter, usually headed by a dean; some cathedral churches, moreover, now have a lay administrator, thereby freeing the dean and clergy increasingly for liturgical and pastoral matters. There is wide consensus that this is a sensible development given the increasing importance of these wonderful buildings, of their human aspect and far-reaching ministry. In addition to the tremendous number of volunteers (15,000 or so), from bellringers to welcomers among the many lay people, the vergers (the 'front line' men and women), the architect, masons and their teams obviously have important duties, and the Masters of the Music (male and female), organists and sometimes organ scholars, train the choirs. An encouraging development has been the introduction of girls' choirs. There are still over thirty cathedral choir schools educating young choristers in the subjects of a normal school curriculum as well as in music. Not all cathedrals have choir schools but they nonetheless still succeed in maintaining a high musical standard, an essential part of cathedral worship. Such cathedrals usually have choirs made up of young people who attend ordinary schools during the day, as opposed to cathedral choir schools, which are residential. Not only the regular daily choral worship but also the long-running weekly BBC radio broadcasts of choral evensong from cathedrals help to ensure that this unique and valued musical tradition, part of Britain's cultural heritage, is more widely appreciated and preserved. Furthermore, projects such as 'Be a chorister for a day' and 'Sing up' are designed to encourage young people to enjoy singing and join choirs.

ORIGINS OF CATHEDRALS

Certain cathedrals were once parts of monasteries. When Henry VIII closed down these establishments in the 1530s (the Dissolution), such cathedrals were refounded by the king and given a new status, staffed by a dean and chapter rather than by a prior and monks. The last prior often became the first dean. They became cathedrals of the 'New Foundation'.

The ones so affected were Canterbury, Carlisle, Durham, Ely, Norwich, Rochester, Winchester and Worcester.

To these were added a few more churches which had never been cathedrals but which were part of monasteries, staffed by an abbot and monks. The last abbot usually became the first dean of the 'New Foundation'. Cathedrals of this type are Bristol, Chester, Gloucester, Oxford and Peterborough.

Some cathedrals were never part of monastic establishments (although the existence of cloisters often gives the impression that they were). They are known as cathedrals of the 'Old Foundation', run by a body of clergy known as canons. The canons were often called *secular*, that is 'of the world', as opposed to monks who were of a closed order in a monastery. This group comprises Bangor, Chichester, Exeter, Hereford, Lichfield, Lincoln, Llandaff, London (St Paul's), St Asaph, St David's, Salisbury, Wells and York.

Certain cathedrals received their status in the nineteenth and twentieth centuries. They were parish churches or specially endowed churches called collegiate churches. Today some of these are known as parish church cathedrals. Here is the list of cathedrals of 'Modern Foundation' beginning with the year 1836: Ripon, Manchester, St Albans, Truro, Liverpool, Newcastle, Southwell, Wakefield; and in the twentieth century, Southwark, Birmingham, Chelmsford, St Edmundsbury, Sheffield, Coventry, Bradford, Newport, Brecon, Blackburn, Leicester, Derby, Guildford, Portsmouth. These new cathedrals were founded in areas where industry and population were on the increase.

A WORD IN GENERAL

We talk of 'parish' or 'abbey' churches. However the term 'cathedral church' is not often used (though correct) – we simply say 'cathedral'.

Our cathedrals when compared with those in mainland Europe, especially in France and Spain, are often distinguished by their great length as opposed to height and also they usually boast a distinctive central tower. They are often, but not always, set within a close, somewhat apart and secluded from busy city centres.

These beautiful buildings, dubbed the *flagships* and *shop windows* of the Christian faith, are appreciated by people of faith and of none, indeed, by all who value beauty and excellence in craftsmanship. They are obviously expensive to maintain since air pollution, traffic and, it is said, the feet of millions of tourists, have a detrimental effect on the ancient stonework, furnishings and flooring. Although often referred to as 'national shrines' our cathedrals are not usually financed by the state. However, recent government funding of several millions of pounds has enabled Anglican as well as Roman Catholic cathedrals both to carry out urgent repairs and to develop strategies in order to function better

Guildford Cathedral from the south-west. Founded in 1936 and uniquely dedicated to the Holy Spirit, the cathedral stands prominently on Stag Hill.

as active hubs within the communities they serve. There are also the indispensable Cathedral Grants Scheme of English Heritage and the Heritage Lottery Fund and the donations of appreciative visitors and worshippers in response to the many appeals.

All this means that a cathedral, whose heart-throb is prayer and worship, is better able to reach out to welcome those seeking solace, the vulnerable and the marginalised and to 'connect people with the sacred', the many who are spiritual and who believe but do not belong to any Church. Moreover, a cathedral's relationship with the parishes in its diocese is frequently explored and with the many challenges, there is much to celebrate.

Cathedrals are held in trust not only for all Christian denominations, but for everyone who may come looking and seeking. To this end the millennium gave impetus to much renovation and conservation and to progress in pastoral, cultural and educational spheres. In recent years cathedrals have learnt to promote themselves more effectively by having special projects and appeals and by developing visitors' centres with interactive displays and exhibitions which inform and enrich one's experience.

It has been said that our ancient cathedrals are the highest expression of the creative art of western Europe. It is essential that our generation, in seeking to further the greater glory of God, should use these buildings imaginatively and for the greater good of all: the worshippers, the many appreciative visitors (over 11 million in 2014 and increasing) and to attract those who have not yet discovered the full potential of these vital centres of Christian witness. Cathedrals are said to be 'open spaces of spiritual possibility' – to quote the Grubb Institute and Theos report: Spiritual Capital.

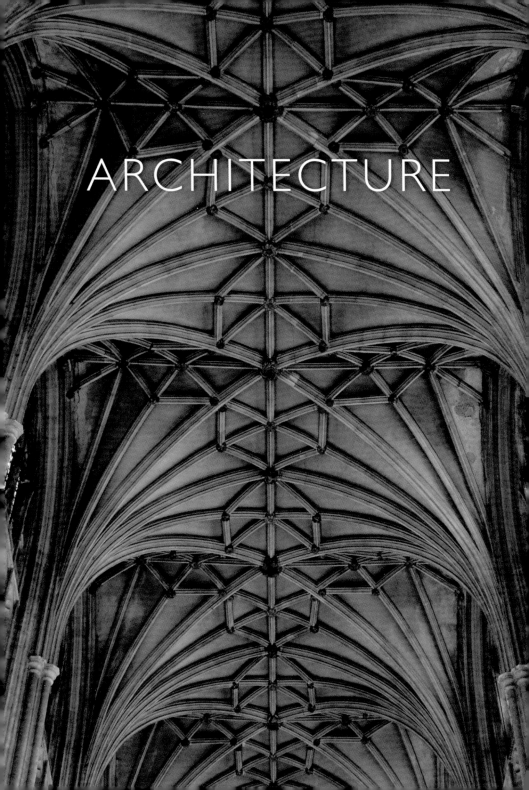

ARCHITECTURE

IT WAS NOT BUILT IN A DAY

THERE ARE VARIOUS styles or periods of architecture which overlap considerably and it is difficult to say exactly when one style ends and another begins. They differ in expression from one country to another, even from one district to another. For the purpose of this book we are concerned mainly with the architectural styles of Britain of the past nine hundred years.

The term *Gothic* occurs frequently. The Goths were a barbaric people who ravaged Europe 1500 years ago, destroying the ancient world and its learning and bringing in the 'Dark Ages'. The word Gothic was first used only a few hundred years ago to describe the architecture of the thirteenth to sixteenth centuries, which, although now seen as remarkable and beautiful, was at one time considered 'barbaric', different and unlike the ancient classical styles of Greece and Rome which had withstood the tests of time. The period we call the Middle Ages, when the Gothic cathedrals were built, was indeed the cathedral age just as the present time is the computer age. Stone was *the* material. The mason and his craft became highly respected, and we still admire and preserve the work of these great craftsmen.

As we travel through Britain we are never far away from a church, abbey or cathedral. To understand styles of architecture we need to go and look, to explore, to discover for ourselves. Any one of the main British cathedrals can display a wide variety of styles since it was probably built, enlarged, lovingly and unlovingly restored over hundreds of years. Nevertheless there is a unity, an artistry and, usually, a happy compromise in the blending of the styles which is typically British.

Previous page: The awe-inspiring columns and lierne vaulting in the nave of Canterbury Cathedral are the work of the famous mason Henry Yevele and are in the Perpendicular style of the late fourteenth century.

LOOKING FOR CLUES

Through the centuries there have been various styles of architecture and special features often arose out of the need to solve structural problems. Vaulted ceilings with stone ribs were developed in some places as an alternative to the wooden roofs which, in Norman churches especially, were constant fire risks. Indeed, many did go up in flames. In the course of time vaults became increasingly elaborate in design and extremely daring in construction, such as very beautiful lierne (tying) rib vaulting, creating star effects and later the stunning 'fan' vaulting of the English Perpendicular period. Examples include Ely (page 35), Winchester (page 42–3), Exeter (page 114), Gloucester (pages 117, 118–19), Norwich (page 160), and Oxford (pages 164–5, 166).

The so-called flying buttress was devised to give added support to walls which had to support higher vaults – for examples see Norwich (page 161) and York (page 166).

Windows also offer many clues as to the period when a church was built. For example, Saxon and Norman churches had thick walls and windows were at first little more than slits, as in a castle. Windows gradually grew in size until the walls themselves almost became 'walls of glass' (see Gloucester, page 118–19; and Carlisle, page 85)

Mouldings (decorative stone bands or strips) also help to date a building – Norman chevron or zig zag, Early English Gothic such as Dog Tooth – four leaves set pyramid-fashion which at an angle look like a dog's tooth! Later, fourteenth-century mouldings known as 'ball flower' are more decorative, and other masonry shows the craftsman's skill at carving elaborate foliage. For some examples of these see Hereford (pages 24 and 126), Durham (page 106–7), and Southwell (pages 209 and 211).

A typical cruciform cathedral plan, comprising corner towers at the west end, a long nave, a transept and crossing (with tower above), then the choir, high altar and (sometimes) Lady Chapel at the easternmost end.

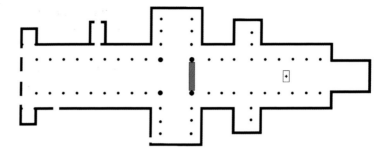

A CATHEDRAL CHURCH – A 'VISUAL AID' PAR EXCELLENCE

The groundplan of a large church (with a small c) is usually in the shape of a cross – *cruciform* – which symbolises the Body of Christ – that is the Church (with a capital C). This is really the people, the *living stones* of the *household of faith,* together with the Holy Trinity – God the Father, God the Son and God the Holy Spirit – the three in one. The Father is the Master Builder, the Son is especially associated with the High Altar in the Sanctuary where the sacrament of Holy Communion celebrates his Death, Resurrection and Ascension, often highlighted by an impressive reredos or backing behind the High Altar (see Liverpool, page 142) and an impressive east window (see Gloucester, page 118–19; Carlisle, page 85) towards the rising sun. The Holy Spirit pervades the whole building, steeped in centuries of prayer and worship up to our present acts of faith and devotions. There are reminders, too, of life's journey: the font for baptism, the lectern (often of 'eagle' design) and the pulpit, both for public reading and preaching of the Bible for spiritual guidance. The Bible and other stories are often depicted in stained glass windows. While a tower symbolizes refuge and fortitude, a spire, pointing heavenwards, alludes to human aspirations expressed in prayer and praise. The east end of the church is the most sacred part where tombs or the shrine of the local saint were placed (for example Canterbury, page 78; Chichester, page 93; Durham, page 105; St Albans, page 184; St David's, page 190) while at the west end, a magnificent window towards the setting sun may represent Eternity and Christ's Second Coming, a memorial, even, to those who have died (for example York Minster, page 32; Gloucester (below); St Asaph, page 189.

***

In ancient times and especially in the so-called Middle Ages, the universe was regarded as the House of God, his dwelling place. By inference, a great church like a cathedral symbolised it too. The basic shape in most cases was a cross – 'cruciform' – to represent Jesus Christ, God Incarnate, here on earth.

The nave and west window at Gloucester Cathedral – Romanesque columns contrast with the later Perpendicular roof vaulting and window, containing still later Victorian glasswork, each built upon the work of previous generations' craftsmen.

Here is a hallowed space with the Vault of Heaven above it, set in time but expressing eternity. For people living in simple wooden houses which were little more than hovels, a cathedral was indeed a vision of Heaven. For us in the twenty-first century there is an opportunity to rediscover something of the awe and wonder such a building as a cathedral can evoke as we stand, stare and worship. A simple stroll around can become a spiritual pilgrimage, an experience which may linger to enrich and inspire long after leaving the building.

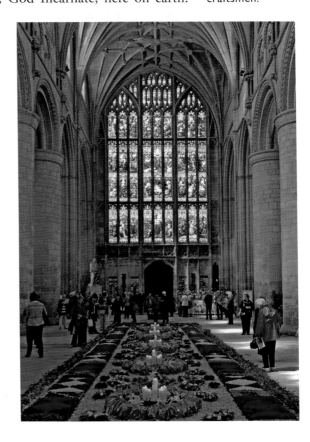

SAXON ROMANESQUE ARCHITECTURE

THE GREEKS AND Romans were erecting grand buildings over two thousand years ago. Following the evacuation of Roman armed forces from Britain soon after AD 400 the country was plunged into a period of upheaval when almost every vestige of civilisation was destroyed or left to decay. These were the Dark Ages, which lasted over five hundred years. Surprisingly, however, this was also the time of the great heroes of the Christian Church; the reign of Alfred the Great was notable for its revival of art and learning, and monasteries were the guardians of culture. Monks and nuns worshipped and worked for the welfare of the people, but few of their Saxon churches remain. Their style of building is called Saxon Romanesque, because it used the Roman rounded arch, as does the Norman style which followed. Churches were often in the style of the Roman basilica with rounded eastern apse. Very few Saxon Romanesque features remain in Britain's cathedrals. At St Albans, where there was probably a Saxon church of considerable size, the little Saxon pillars, or balusters, have been reused high up at the transept crossing. Also at St Albans the Norman tower is faced with tiles from the Roman town of Verulamium nearby, which are almost as old as Christianity itself. Much of the fabric is from the deserted Roman town.

Beneath Ripon Cathedral is a unique Saxon crypt, the oldest part of any British cathedral. The Saxon church built by Bishop Wilfrid *c.*672 was said to be one of the finest stone buildings in northern Europe. It was destroyed by Viking pirates but the crypt, built for the display of sacred relics, has survived and can still be visited today.

Saxon work can be detected in several places if one looks carefully. More often than not, however, it has been heavily disguised or covered up with more recent work. In most places where there is a great church or cathedral standing today there is evidence of a Christian church of some kind on the site from Saxon times.

NORMAN ARCHITECTURE

T HE NORMANS, LED by Duke William, conquered England in 1066 and in the years immediately following, but several fine churches of no mean size had been built in England before this by Norman masons. However, the Norman building drive after 1066 was tremendous and it left a permanent mark on English architecture. Many cathedrals have Norman Romanesque work somewhere. First and foremost is Durham Cathedral, the finest and least spoiled Norman Romanesque church in Europe. By 1133, after only about forty years of building, the cathedral had been completed. The superb nave pillars with their bold incised patterns make an unforgettable impact as one enters. The Norman church ended in an apse, as was the normal custom then, but at Durham, as in most places, the cathedral was later enlarged eastwards. This fine, massive church, on its impressive site above the horseshoe loop of the river Wear, has three great towers; these are Norman at the lower level but were later increased in height.

At Peterborough, the least spoiled of great Norman churches after Durham, the curved apse behind the high altar remains. The eye is led to it along the impressive sweep of the Norman nave arcade, the choir, central tower, transepts and presbytery. The absence of any screen across the church makes for a unique uninterrupted view eastwards.

Norwich, too, still possesses its Norman apse with radiating chapels – the chevet – as in a French church. In the whole of Europe, moreover, there are few cathedrals in which the once traditional placing of the bishop's throne at the centre of the apse, east of the high altar, remains to this day as at Norwich. Subsequent architectural additions blend well

Opposite: Massive and dignified, the two west towers of Durham Cathedral, each 144 feet high. The upper surfaces are covered with decoration in the form of arcading.

At Hereford Cathedral zig-zag and scrollwork motifs are typical late Romanesque features; the cylindrical piers are Norman Romanesque, common here in the West Country.

with the Norman core. The central tower, with a spire added later, has attractive Norman decoration.

Like Peterborough and Norwich, Ely also has a long and impressive nave. This most beautiful cathedral, once called the Norman Lady as opposed to the Norman Lord at Durham, is built, surprisingly, on solid rock, in the flat marshy fenlands. The fascinating carving round the outside of the prior's door (see page 108) is a superb example of Norman Romanesque art.

There are fine crypts at Canterbury, Gloucester, Rochester and York, but the most notable is at Worcester, with its forest of pillars, all part of the original Norman church. Here there is an early example of a central pillar with several arches radiating from it, an idea that appeared later in the Worcester chapter house, the forerunner of many circular or polygonal chapter houses with central pillars. The chapter house and vestibule at Bristol are especially good examples of Norman work with a wealth of decoration.

At Gloucester and Hereford there are cylindrical pillars, a marked feature of Norman building in the west. The Hereford pillars and arches are late Norman with some very elaborate carving. Original Norman work is also still to be seen in the south transept here. At Winchester it is in the north transept where the solid fortress-like Norman architecture particularly impresses, especially when one considers that the great church was built on a raft of logs in a marsh! The Norman nave is still there, too, but unseen. One cannot but wonder at the way in which the later Gothic builders here completely encased the Norman structure in a Gothic covering instead of pulling down and rebuilding as, for example, at Canterbury.

The first central tower at Winchester collapsed in 1107 and had to be replaced, but at St Albans the tower, built of Roman bricks and tiles (see page 21), is a fine example of Norman strength. Central towers are a marked feature of British cathedrals: almost all have one, but this is not the case in other countries. Exeter, an exception, has retained its Norman towers, one on each side of the church at the transept crossing, and this is unusual. The superb Norman tower at Bury St Edmunds stands apart from the cathedral since it was originally the gateway in front of the now ruined abbey. It has been described as the finest Norman building in Britain.

The Norman Romanesque style, solid-looking and massive, aptly conveyed the strength and fortitude of the Christian Church. As early as 1096, however, only thirty years after the Conquest, the earliest stone rib-vaulted ceiling was built at Durham. A hundred years after this daring and momentous advance the pointed arch was gaining ground so that in the late twelfth century the beginnings of Gothic architecture, the Norman Transitional, appeared in Britain. This was a gradual process and in some places building was still progressing in the Norman style until late in the twelfth century. Examples of this transitional style are at Canterbury, Ripon, Rochester and Worcester.

More Norman architecture can be seen at: Canterbury, Carlisle, Chester, Chichester, Lincoln, Llandaff, Newport, Norwich, Oxford, Rochester, St Albans, St David's and Southwell.

Winchester: the main arcade, gallery and clerestory in the North Transept shows what the Norman cathedral was like throughout; unmistakably confident, solid and fortress-like, even though it was built on a marsh.

EARLY ENGLISH GOTHIC

In 1140 the foundation stone of the new abbey church of St Denis, on the outskirts of Paris, was laid. Abbot Suger, the designer of St Denis, wanted people to be uplifted in heart and mind and to this end he designed a church of great beauty and richness of decoration.

The Gothic style evolved in the region around Paris known as the Ile de France. The pointed arch was known in the Middle East, but its introduction into European architecture profoundly affected the atmosphere of church buildings. In contrast to the Norman or Romanesque church, where the emphasis is horizontal and 'down to earth', the Gothic church is designed to draw the eyes of the worshipper upwards. Walls occupy a smaller space to allow for more and larger windows to let in plenty of light. Pillars become more and more slender, extremely tall clusters of stone rods, supporting high soaring arches and daring vaulted ceilings. In some cathedrals vertical shafts of dark Purbeck marble from Dorset were used abundantly.

Soon after the murder of Thomas à Becket in 1170 in his own cathedral at Canterbury, and after a fire there, work began on rebuilding the eastern end of the cathedral to house a shrine to the archbishop. A Frenchman, William of Sens, was the master mason. After an unfortunate scaffolding accident which left him a cripple, he had to hand the work over to another William, an Englishman. The shrine of St Thomas has since been removed but the choir and Trinity Chapel remain, early examples of the Gothic style in Britain.

The earliest expression of Gothic architecture in England is usually called Early English and it covers approximately the period 1200 to 1300. Architects and builders in England

Canterbury: in the Choir the beginnings of the Early English Gothic style still indicate a strong hint of the earlier Romanesque. The terms Romanesque and Gothic were not known then, of course. Gothic was first used as a derogatory term in the late seventeenth century.

began to develop their own ideas and styles and three cathedrals that demonstrate this change are Wells, Salisbury and Lincoln.

At Wells the building of the cathedral in the Early English style was begun about 1180 and continued for about sixty years. The nave pillars have a very solid look about them, by no means Norman but nevertheless the clusters of slender shafts form quite massive piers.

In 1220 at Old Sarum, the original Norman settlement at Salisbury, Bishop Poore (later Bishop of Durham) obtained permission to move the Christian community away from the unpleasant and cramped site near the castle to a lower level on the banks of the river Avon, where water was more plentiful. The cathedral at New Sarum was built for the most part according to the original design, and within the short period of just under forty years, in the Early English Gothic style. Certain parts, including the world-famous spire, were added later. In the nave there is abundant use of Purbeck marble (seen earlier at Canterbury), helping to create a stately, precise impact, somewhat plain and cold. The lancet style of window can be seen throughout the building and is typical of this early Gothic style in England.

Opposite: Salisbury's elegant thirteenth-century west front is enriched with sculptures (some of them Victorian replacements) arranged rank upon rank; there is an attractive symmetry about it.

In 1192 Bishop Hugh, who came from Avalon in France, supervised the start of the rebuilding of Lincoln Cathedral after an earth tremor in 1185. His influence, though enormous, was short-lived because he died before the turn of the century and the work was carried forward by others, notably Bishop Robert Grosseteste. The eastern end of the cathedral was built in the form of a chevet, French-style, but this was later replaced by the famous Angel Choir with its beautiful carvings, including the endearing Lincoln imp. Purbeck marble was extensively used throughout.

Notable Early English west fronts can be seen at Salisbury, Wells, Peterborough and Ripon. At Peterborough, where the west front is kept perpendicular to the Norman building by

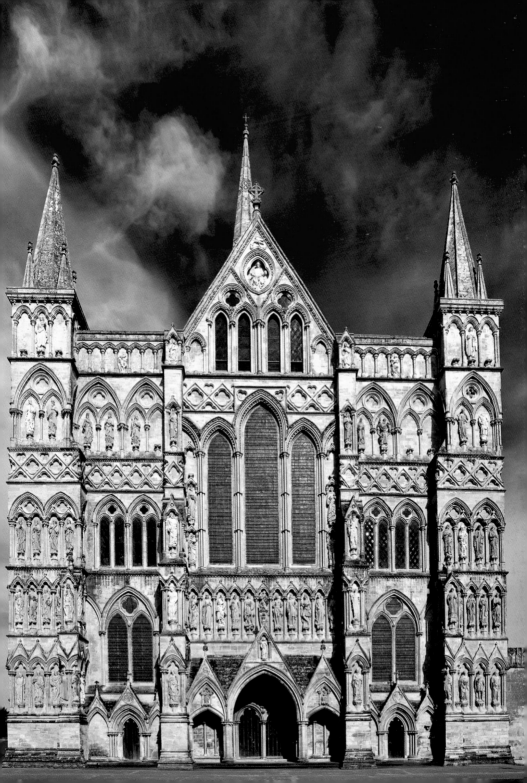

Wells: the clustered piers in the nave. This is the first Gothic church in England in which the pointed arch was used throughout, with hardly any French influence.

giant steel rods within the thick walls, there are three 80 foot high arches forming a unique and magnificent façade. The Ripon west front is much smaller and somewhat plain, the marked feature here being the characteristically Early English lancet windows. Pride of place, however, is taken by the west front at Wells, the finest in England, nearly 150 feet wide, comprising an impressive panorama of statues. There are prophets, saints, kings and other carvings to instruct the medieval worshipper (and his present-day counterpart). Several of the figures are life-size and larger, but unfortunately many are in a damaged state. Restoration, although backed by scholarship and research, has taken place amidst controversy but it is no less a masterpiece.

Just as Norman architecture of the eleventh and twelfth centuries had embodied the aspirations of the Church militant, so Gothic architecture of the thirteenth century and after conveys the feeling of release and *joie de vivre*, the aspirations of a Church triumphant. In a Gothic church one cannot but be uplifted.

Features of the Early English period can also be seen at: Brecon, Bristol, Chichester, Ely, Hereford, Rochester, St Albans, St David's, Southwark, Worcester and York (note especially here the tall Early English lancet windows, the 'Five Sisters', at the transept crossing). At Westminster Abbey (not a cathedral) important new work with marked French influence was carried out at the time of Henry III on this royal church. The king was a Francophile and the extremely high vault and chevet-style east end set the abbey apart from English cathedrals.

The impressive statuary on the west front at Wells Cathedral.

MID GOTHIC OR DECORATED

IT IS DIFFICULT to imagine fully the original beauty of many of Britain's churches. Damage caused by image breakers and restorers has often ruined the original impact which they must have had on local worshippers and pilgrims. For the most part we are deprived of the gilding and the colour of church interiors.

Exeter Cathedral is England's finest 'Decorated' cathedral. The nave is not very high since its height was determined by the twin Norman towers at the transepts which were incorporated into the new building. The splendid vaulted ceiling has been likened to branching trees and it is continuous from west to east, a distance of 300 feet. With no central tower to break the continuity, it is thus unique and one of the finest cathedral roofs and certainly the longest unbroken Gothic vault in the world. With a pair of binoculars one can see more effectively the beautifully carved ceiling bosses which were designed to cover the meeting points of the ribs in the vaulting. Vaulting, with its additional little link-up ribs called liernes, and bosses are both notable features of the Decorated style. At Exeter there is everywhere elaborate, delicate carving in corbels and bosses and expert craftsmanship in wood and stone. The window tracery – patterns formed by stonework – is also a product of this period and both the east and west windows at Exeter are fine examples. Window tracery became more and more beautiful and complex during the Decorated period.

It is Carlisle Cathedral, however, which possesses what is justly claimed to be the finest traceried window in England. It is very large and forms a superb eastern climax to the choir and high altar. The tracery of the east window immediately above the high altar at Ripon is also very fine. The west window at York Minster is aptly called 'the Heart of Yorkshire', dating from

Opposite: York Minster's fine West Window has early glass (as elsewhere in the building) and stone tracery in the Curvilinear Decorated Style crafted (1338–9) by the same mason who designed Carlisle's superb East Window (page 85) The heart shape – dubbed the Heart of Yorkshire – may represent the Sacred Heart of Christ, reminding medieval pilgrims (and us) of God's love for humankind. The East Window is even more exceptional.

At Ely the unique Octagon (1332), contains the only Gothic dome, crowning the earlier nave and presbytery, an unforgettable sight across the Fens.

1338. The nave here is also in the Decorated style and is the widest and highest in England. As a result, except in the side aisles, there is unfortunately no stone vault. The chapter house is vast, with notable geometrical traceried windows and many weird and wonderful carvings on the stall canopies. Yet more wonderful is the fact that, for all its size, there is no central pillar. A stone vault was intended but a wooden roof was built instead.

Some of the finest stone carvings of the period are those which adorn the smaller chapter house at Southwell Minster, Nottinghamshire's village cathedral. There are birds and animals among foliage – the famous 'Leaves of Southwell', a superb example of medieval craftsmanship.

Work on the nave at Worcester was interrupted by the Black Death and the demands of the French wars and so there are pillars in the Decorated style on one side and later Gothic on the other side, when work was resumed.

A staggering achievement of these years was accomplished at Ely Cathedral: the erection of its unique Octagon – the only Gothic dome and one of the most incredible engineering feats of the Middle Ages. This was built in 1332 to replace a central Norman tower which had fallen in a storm ten years before. The oak structure supports 400 tons of wood and lead. Eight oak corner posts, each over 60 feet high, form the framework of the lantern, which seems almost to hang above our heads. The Lady Chapel at Ely is also a very remarkable building, possessing the widest vaulted ceiling of the period, a gentle curve nearly 50 feet across. If only we could still see this unique chapel in all its original colour and beauty in windows and sculpture, but it is unfortunately one of those many places that suffered at the hands of Civil War soldiery.

At Salisbury in the mid fourteenth century the central tower and spire were completed, to a height of just over 400 feet; the total weight is 6400 tons. At Lincoln there was once a spire on the central tower, itself the highest medieval tower in England (just over 270 feet), and with the spire it reached a height of nearly 525 feet, the tallest in Europe. A storm in the mid sixteenth century destroyed that.

By 1350 the very high Lady Chapel at Lichfield was completed to rehouse the shrine of St Chad. The west front dates from about 1300 and the three famous spires, unique to Lichfield and familiarly known as the 'Ladies of the Vale', originated in this Decorated period, but these and the rest of the building have been considerably restored. The Lady Chapel at Wells, and its subsequent link with the rest of the cathedral by means of a retro-choir beyond the high altar, are extremely

Ely has a stunning Lady Chapel (1321–73) – the largest and, uniquely, it is almost detached from the cathedral itself; it has the widest medieval vault, a ceiling spanning 50 feet; most cathedrals have a Lady Chapel, so called in honour of Our Lady, the Virgin Mary, Mother of Jesus.

beautiful. This Lady Chapel has an unusual octagonal shape with one of the finest lierne vaults. The retro-choir, with its slender Purbeck marble shafts, was perhaps built for a shrine, following the fashion of the time, but no local saint was forthcoming. This reminds us that most of the extensive building drive of these years was made possible by money given by pilgrims. This was the age of pilgrimages and some cathedrals were more fortunate in the way of tombs, shrines and relics than others. Nevertheless work went on apace at Wells linking the eastern extension with the choir and the presbytery, which was also rebuilt in the same century. The east window, the Golden Window above the high altar, is one of the finest in England. This part of Wells Cathedral, with its feeling of light and space, is more characteristic of the Perpendicular style which was to follow towards the end of the century.

The beautiful chapter house at Wells, reached by climbing a unique flight of steps, was completed in the early 1300s. It has a superb vault radiating from a slender central pillar. The geometrical windows are decorated with ballflower ornamentation. Such mouldings are common in the Decorated style of the fourteenth century. In the nave the famous inverted arches of scissor design in the form of a cross were inserted about 1340 to strengthen the central tower. This tower is, for the most part, of the Decorated Gothic period.

Thirty-two ribs radiate in palm-tree fashion from the clustered shaft of the central column of the very beautiful octagonal chapter house at Wells Cathedral.

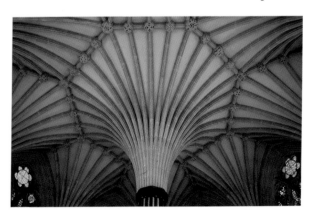

It is on the exterior of the central tower at Hereford that the use of ballflower adornment is so pronounced. We have seen that central towers are a vital and prominent feature of almost all English cathedrals, and in the fourteenth and fifteenth centuries most of them were built or rebuilt as money came in from visiting pilgrims. This is the case at Hereford, where offerings were made at the shrine of St Thomas Cantelupe. There will be more about central towers in the next chapter but it should be mentioned that Decorated towers of the fourteenth century were originally designed to have spires, which have since disappeared.

In the early 1370s work was started at Gloucester on renovating the cloisters. As yet this was not a cathedral but here we meet the earliest fan-vault of any note. The fan-vault was to be a highlight of the style of architecture which was to develop within the following 150 years or so.

The fourteenth century was no easy time to live because the Hundred Years War with France began (1337) and the dreaded plague, the Black Death (1348–9), spread across Europe, killing thousands and halving the population in some parts of England. It took its toll of craftsmen and labourers and held up building operations on many a church and cathedral. In spite of these setbacks, however, the fourteenth century was notable for many great achievements in architecture and for its embellishment with exquisite carving in wood and stone and elaborate window tracery.

A feature sometimes found is a maze, symbolising pilgrimage; such inspirational floor designs are more common in mainland Europe. However, temporary mazes are often created as part of a special event like a festival. Ely Cathedral has a rare (for Britain) unicursal maze in the floor of the west tower.

In addition to the examples already mentioned in this chapter, the following cathedrals possess notable work of the Decorated period: Bristol, Chester, Chichester, St Albans, St Asaph, St David's and Winchester.

Hereford Cathedral's central tower boasted a lead-covered timber spire until 1790; however, with corner pinnacles added in the 1830s, this tower of the Decorated period, with typical ball-flower ornamentation, still rises impressively over this city by the river Wye.

LATE GOTHIC: THE PERPENDICULAR STYLE

THE FINEST EXPRESSIONS of the Perpendicular style are not to be found in cathedrals at all. The chapel of King's College in Cambridge is the best example, and numerous parish churches up and down England are built in the style. St Edmundsbury Cathedral is largely a Perpendicular church, but with a modern extension, of which more will be said later. Many wonderful parish churches of the period can be seen in the Cotswolds and East Anglia. Both these districts were noted for their sheep farming and its allied trades. England's trade in wool grew in importance during the latter part of the Middle Ages. The Black Death caused landowners to turn to sheep farming since labour was short and only a few men were needed to care for the flocks. Sheep farmers and wool merchants became very rich. In towns they built many fine houses and, most important of all, they spent vast sums of money on building and furnishing some very beautiful churches, many of which are of cathedral-like proportions. Appropriately, one wool merchant had these words set in stained glass: 'I thank my God and ever shall, it is the sheep hath paid for all.'

The Perpendicular style is the third phase of Gothic architecture in England. It was also an English invention, peculiar to this country. While European architecture became more and more flamboyant, often with extreme adornment, in England the new style was clean-cut, restrained and lofty. Another appropriate name for the style is 'rectilinear'. In the hands of ever more ambitious designers and masons churches became frameworks of stone with extensive window areas filled with stained glass.

It was mentioned in the last chapter that the fan-vault appeared in the new cloisters at Gloucester in the 1370s.

Although lacking the usual pinnacles, the early fifteenth-century central tower at York Minster is nonetheless dignified and very grand, and the interior floor area is the largest in England. The tower and choir (to the right) are fine examples of the Perpendicular style.

Opposite:
The choir and east window in Gloucester Cathedral heralded a new architectural experience: 'walls of glass' culminating in the largest stone-traceried window in England (erected about 1350). Its sides are set at an angle to allow for more glass and the easternmost bays of the choir slope outwards to accommodate this. It is really a war memorial to those who fell at the battle of Crécy (1346) and the siege of Calais (1347).

Work had started earlier on the redesign of the Norman east end, beginning with the south transept. Fortunately for the monks of the then abbey of St Peter, the cost was met by pilgrims' offerings received at the tomb of King Edward II, who was murdered at Berkeley Castle in 1327 and buried in the abbey. The lierne vault over 90 feet up, the vertical tracery, the lofty mullions or pillars separating the windows and the great windows themselves transformed the Gloucester choir and presbytery into a building full of space and light. The great east window, the largest of its kind in Britain, is now just over 650 years old and contains much of its original glass. Further east still is the delightful Lady Chapel, linked to the main church by the Whispering Gallery, a cleverly contrived bridge. The ambulatory still follows the earlier Norman plan. The work of transforming the choir and presbytery necessitated the insertion of the 'flying arches' at the central tower, which itself was replaced in the mid fifteenth century by the glorious 225 foot tower which stands today.

It is the central tower at Worcester that is the most impressive exterior feature there. Completed in 1374, it really is at the cathedral's centre and this is unusual! It is the earliest of the Perpendicular towers, probably a forerunner of the Gloucester tower, though not so high. The famous central tower at Canterbury, the Bell Harry, was built over a hundred years later, at the end of the fifteenth century. The lantern of this tower has a magnificent fan-vault. At Norman Durham the central tower was increased in height. The work began in 1465. About two-thirds of the way up there are battlements, probably intended to be the top of an earlier design, but which now seem out of place. York Minster is the largest cathedral of the middle ages in Britain. Modern engineering and technology have been employed to strengthen the whole structure. The three towers date from the second half of the fifteenth century. It is unfortunate that

the centre one, completed in 1480, lacks the usual corner pinnacles on the exterior, but the newly restored lantern stone-vault, with nearly one hundred bosses, is breathtaking.

Ceiling bosses and vaults are two notable features of Perpendicular architecture, and Norwich Cathedral has some of the finest examples. Here the Norman nave received its high vault in the 1460s. Work on vaulting the rest of this great Norman church continued for many years. There are hundreds of bosses here and in the cloisters. There is a pleasing blend of Norman and late Gothic, especially at the eastern end, where there are tall Gothic windows and flying buttresses on the exterior. There is added light and a sense of space here, the Norman building being much enhanced by the additional work.

Three major works of the Perpendicular period are the naves at Canterbury and Winchester and the choir at York.

Transformation at Winchester; in the soaring nave the Perpendicular masonry encases the early Norman Romanesque building, to awe-inspiring effect.

At Canterbury the superb Perpendicular nave replaces the earlier Norman one. Here are the familiar tall slender pillars and pointed arches, comprising one of the greatest architectural splendours of the late Middle Ages. It is interesting to compare this nave with the one at Winchester. There again are soaring pillars and arches but at Winchester the Norman structure remains, encased in Perpendicular-style masonry. Bishop William of Wykeham, founder of New College, Oxford, and Winchester College public school, was a famous national

figure of the fourteenth century and he initiated the work at Winchester, although subsequent bishops had a hand in the task as well. Wykeham is commemorated in one of the many chantry chapels for which the cathedral is noted.

Work on the choir at York began in the early 1360s. Lofty and full of light, this eastern end culminates in a great wall of glass. The east window is the largest of its kind still complete with its brilliant glass, made by John Thornton of Coventry in the early 1400s in only three years. The roof of this easternmost

In the nave at Winchester the earlier Norman work (still to be seen in the transepts) was largely retained but encased and hidden (1390s onwards) completely transforming it into a late medieval Gothic masterpiece, a Perpendicular marvel (cf Canterbury). In the foreground is the rare black Tournai marble font (1180s).

end is of wood imitating stone and is a nineteenth-century replacement following a fire started by a mad fire-raiser.

It is perhaps the fan-vault, ingenious and decorative, that leaves the most lasting impressions of delight and wonder. In 1496, over a hundred years after the first fan-vaults in the Gloucester cloisters, the 'new building' beyond the Norman apse at Peterborough was started. Its Perpendicular fan-vaulting was probably by the architect of King's College Chapel, Cambridge, John Wastell. William Orchard's vaulting above the choir and presbytery at Oxford Cathedral (Christ Church) is an array of fan-vaulting, lierne vaulting, bosses and pendants. 'The most beautiful chapel in all Christendom', Henry VII's Chapel in Westminster Abbey, built in the early 1500s, takes the fan-vault to its climax. The very beautiful wooden roof above the nave at St David's Cathedral was built at the end of the fifteenth century. Made of Irish oak, it is a remarkable design of pendant arches, delicately carved.

We have already noted that there are numerous parish churches in the Perpendicular style. Some of these churches have since received cathedral status, notably St Edmundsbury, Manchester and Sheffield. A church which owes much to the Perpendicular period is Ripon Cathedral, sometimes called Ripon Minster, which became a cathedral in 1836. It was partly transformed into a spacious Perpendicular church, but the fifteenth-century builders failed to finish the work. This is especially noticeable at the crossing, where the central tower possesses two round arches from the earlier church and two pointed ones where the transformation was begun – a unique feature.

When comparing the Norman nave arcade at Gloucester with the cathedral's Perpendicular choir and presbytery one realises that, architecturally, we have come a very long way. Here indeed is an object lesson in the two contrasting styles. It is regrettable that there was no purpose-built cathedral exclusively in the Perpendicular style. Although Britain was becoming richer and more independent at this point in her history, more money was being directed towards undertakings other than cathedral churches.

Further Perpendicular features can be seen at: Bath Abbey (no longer a cathedral), Bradford, Chelmsford, Newcastle, St Albans, St Asaph, Wakefield and Worcester.

In St David's Cathedral the late Romanesque nave (1180s) has many unique, beautiful features from later centuries; the rare wooden ceiling of Welsh (Irish?) oak (1530–40) with its intricately carved castle-like pendants gloriously embellishes this wonderful interior.

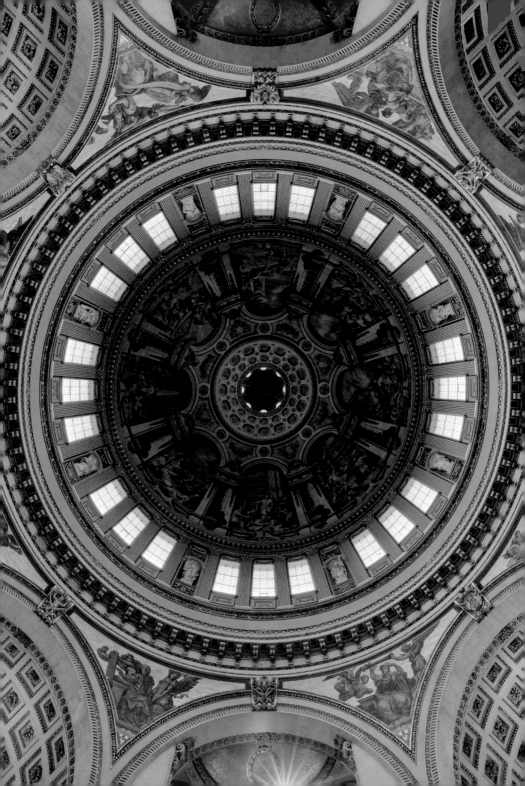

FROM THE RENAISSANCE TO THE GOTHIC REVIVAL

THE SIXTEENTH CENTURY was a time of religious and social upheaval which came fast in the wake of the Reformation. Following Henry VIII's break with Rome, monasteries were closed and many church treasures were commandeered by the Crown. It is not surprising that during this period there was a general decline in church building and especially in cathedral building.

By the seventeenth century old St Paul's Cathedral in London, one of the most splendid and largest of the Gothic cathedrals in Britain, was in an extremely ruinous condition and it was destroyed in the Great Fire of London of 1666. The present St Paul's, which replaces it, is the finest example of English Renaissance church architecture and as such it is unique among British cathedrals. Its designer, Sir Christopher Wren, adapted many Renaissance ideas he had learnt in Europe. A relative of his was Bishop of Ely, and the Octagon there, the only Gothic dome, had no doubt impressed him on his visits to Ely. The term 'Renaissance' means rebirth or revival and refers to the period in history when art was revitalised following the rediscovery of the ancient art of Greece and Rome.

St Paul's Cathedral, largely paid for by a tax on coal entering the Port of London, is built of Portland stone and took just under thirty-five years to complete. Sir Christopher Wren himself, although very old, was present to see the finish. Surmounting the famous dome, an unmistakable landmark, is the cross, its pinnacle 365 feet above the ground. The entrance is approached by an impressive flight of steps to the portico. Inside we see huge round arches, Italian-style, on massive square pillars leading to a vast central area with

Looking up into the dome (consecrated 1710), the 'glory of St Paul's'. There is a hint of Ely's medieval 'Octagon' (page 109), which the architect Sir Christopher Wren knew well. This dome's octagonal central space is 102 feet in diameter. Above this is a hidden inner brick cone and then the iconic dome so unmistakable on London's skyline (see page 147).

eight piers below the dome. The interior of St Paul's is very ornate, enriched with panelling and mosaics, intricate carving by Grinling Gibbons and ironwork by Jean Tijou. The very poignant word *Resurgam* is inscribed on a stone above the south door in the south transept. It means 'I shall rise again'; it is said that Sir Christopher Wren came across the stone in the rubble of Old St Paul's. A new St Paul's certainly did rise and has survived war damage. Like many cathedrals, it now faces enormous expense to protect and maintain it.

In the mid seventeenth century certain cathedrals had suffered extensive damage as a result of the Civil War. Stained glass was smashed; statues were broken; wooden furnishings were burnt on soldiers' fires within the cathedrals themselves; horses were stabled in the buildings, as at St Asaph. After one battle hundreds of prisoners, captured by Oliver Cromwell, were marched to Durham and locked in the cathedral. The choir stalls and other wooden furnishings were burned by the prisoners to keep warm. During the eighteenth century many great cathedrals were sadly neglected and allowed to fall into disrepair. This made restoration necessary in all of them to a greater or lesser degree.

The decaying medieval parish church in Derby (the church of All Saints, a cathedral since 1927) was demolished in 1723, apart from the fine Perpendicular tower. The cathedral is one of the finest early eighteenth-century churches in Britain. The architect was James Gibbs, who also designed St Martin-in-the-Fields in London, and this church is similar to it. In the twentieth century changes were necessary here to allow more space for the better conduct of cathedral worship around the high altar. The new design involved a partial rearrangement of the Bakewell screen, a superb piece of wrought ironwork by a local craftsman.

The Cathedral Church of St Philip in Birmingham, consecrated in 1715, is built in the English Baroque style to the design of the Warwickshire architect Thomas Archer. There

is a gallery on each side of the nave with square fluted columns rising to a flat ceiling. There are stained glass windows designed by Burne-Jones and made by William Morris.

Some cathedrals have unfortunately always been at a disadvantage in regard to the maintenance of their stonework. Sandstone in particular does not withstand the elements well, as cathedrals like Lichfield show only too well.

There were also restorers who did much damage. James Wyatt was nicknamed 'the destroyer' after his work at Salisbury, where stained glass was removed 'because it made the cathedral dark'. Many restorers, however, rendered invaluable service and saved buildings from utter ruin. At St Albans, for example, Lord Grimthorpe financed extensive restoration, although the purist will maintain that Victorian additions and renovation here do not blend with the Norman and Gothic original. This is true in many places but we should

Derby: James Gibbs's nave for the parish church of All Saints, built in 1725. The church became a cathedral in 1927. The splendid wrought-iron screen bearing the Hanoverian royal arms is by Robert Bakewell. There has been considerable refurbishment and redecoration.

nevertheless be grateful for the munificence and enthusiasm of such men, even though it may have sometimes been misplaced. The Victorians were undoubtedly thorough, and their efforts were timely. Lichfield Cathedral needed much restoration and nearly all the statues on the imposing west front are Victorian replacements.

In the nineteenth century a few parish churches in industrial areas were given cathedral status. The fine Perpendicular collegiate church at Manchester (1847) and the fine medieval church at Newcastle (1882) are examples, and both these churches have a long history. Manchester Cathedral was begun in 1422 in the Perpendicular Gothic style. A terrorist bomb nearby in 1992 caused considerable damage, which

The nave bridge at Liverpool Cathedral frames the vista towards the east window.

is now thankfully restored. Unfortunately the beauty of Newcastle had faded during years of neglect, so restoration there, in the fifteenth-century style of the Gothic Revival, was considerable. Blackburn Cathedral, with its tall pillars and pointed arches, was built in this style in the early nineteenth century although it became a cathedral only in 1926. Modern alterations include an impressive central space and a lantern tower. At Bristol plans to replace the Norman nave during the Middle Ages were never fulfilled and the present nave was completed in 1888 in the appropriate fourteenth-century style. Leicester Cathedral, considerably restored over the years, has a broach spire, rebuilt in the 1860s, unique for a cathedral.

A crown of light at St Albans. In September 1989 Diana, Princess of Wales, unveiled the newly glazed 'Rose' by Alan Younger. The window (Victorian tracery) dates from Lord Grimthorpe's restoration.

The nave at Southwark was restored and completed in 1897. This church had been falling into ruin and the development of the railway at London Bridge threatened its very existence. There is Norman work here and some exceptionally fine Gothic work, especially in the transepts, the choir and the beautiful retro-choir beyond the high altar screen. Here on the south bank of the Thames this cathedral stands in a most unlikely but perhaps not unfortunate position. Though cramped by warehouses and thoroughfares, Southwark Cathedral reminds us that the Church has an important part to play in a busy modern world.

As has been noted already Lord Grimthorpe spent much time, energy and, most of all, money to 'save' St Albans Abbey (later the Cathedral). A hundred years or so later his 'rose' window was to be beautified.

THE TWENTIETH CENTURY

TRURO IS ONE of four Anglican cathedrals in Britain completed in the twentieth century. The style chosen by the architect, John Pearson, was Early English of the thirteenth century. The building, completed in 1910, is therefore very much 'out of period'. Part of the parish church of St Mary was incorporated into the new design (the rest was demolished). The cathedral has interesting features and its three spires make an impressive skyline.

Liverpool Cathedral is also Gothic in conception with high soaring arches and a vault. Sir Giles Gilbert Scott's prize-winning design was conceived in the early 1900s when he was twenty-two and it has of necessity been modified over the years. He did not live to see its completion. The lasting impression is one of vastness; a congregation of several thousand can be seated so that each person has an uninterrupted view of the proceedings. This is partly due to the absence of pillars. The building is of local sandstone and was completed in the 1970s. It is the largest cathedral in Britain and among the five largest in the world.

Liverpool and Guildford are the only Anglican cathedrals built on new sites in Britain since the Middle Ages. The central tower at Guildford is at the highest point of the hill. The design of the cathedral again follows the medieval pattern – with one vital difference. Unlike medieval worship, modern practice prefers an uninterrupted view of the high altar. There is therefore no screen across this church as was the pattern in old churches and, to quote the architect, Sir Edward Maufe RA, 'the seven ... simple ... arches on each side lead us forward in spirit ...'. The symbol of the cathedral is the Guildford Cross, in the shape of the building, incorporating extra arms at the base, the welcoming arms of the Church symbolised by the unique west front.

Completed in 1962, Coventry Cathedral, north of the ruins of the medieval church destroyed in 1942, is linked by an impressive porch. The nave is seen here but the full impact of the stained glass is seen only from the choir and sanctuary; in place of an 'east' window, Graham Sutherland's tapestry, the largest in the world, is an awe-inspiring climax depicting Christ in Majesty.

Coventry Cathedral is a building very much of the mid twentieth century. It was designed by Sir Basil Spence. Lying north to south, the cathedral was completed in 1962 and covers the area north of the old cathedral destroyed in 1941. An impressive porch links the old ruins with the new building. Angels and saints are engraved on the huge 'west' window. From this point the eye is drawn to the high altar and, in place of the usual 'east' window, to the largest tapestry in the world, depicting Christ in Majesty. Designed by Graham Sutherland, it was woven in France. The baptistery window, a blaze of colour, is another memorable feature. The nave windows are set at an unusual angle so that their impact is experienced fully only from the sanctuary. There is much symbolism in the various architectural features and furnishings. The Cross of Nails and the Charred Cross of Coventry in the ruined part are both poignant reminders of reconciliation, one of the main tasks facing the Christian Church today. Jacob Epstein's sculpture 'St Michael and the Devil' is just outside the entrance.

At Llandaff there has been a similar 'resurrection' after the land-mine damage of 1941. The most outstanding modern feature is Jacob Epstein's 'Majestas' in unpolished aluminium, on a concrete arch-cum-pulpitum designed to allow an uninterrupted view the length of the cathedral, but at the same time punctuating the traditional division between nave and choir.

Modern extension work has been carried out at Derby, Portsmouth, Sheffield and St Edmundsbury cathedrals. At Portsmouth parts of the building recall late Norman and early Gothic origins. In the seventeenth century the tower and nave, damaged in the Civil War, were rebuilt by order of Charles II. Now this ancient church has been refashioned in keeping with its new cathedral status. The late-twentieth-century work draws on elements of earlier styles. There has been sensitive reordering and impressive new work at Blackburn, Bradford and Chelmsford and at Wakefield there are now attractive precincts.

At Sheffield the new section is very extensive – almost a completely new church. Work has been carried out on the nave, St George's Chapel, a further tower and a narthex (a kind of porch) and a chapel to the Holy Spirit.

In 1970, the 1100th anniversary of the martyrdom of King Edmund of East Anglia, the new eastward extension of St Edmundsbury Cathedral was consecrated. The cathedral today is also the parish church of St James, originally built, together with two other churches, for the townsfolk to worship in away from the monks at the abbey, whose ruins lie behind the cathedral. This is no doubt one reason why the abbey itself did not become the parish church as it did elsewhere, such as at St Albans. The tall slender pillars of the nave at St Edmundsbury make it a particularly fine example of the work of John Wastell, who lived in Bury St Edmunds until his death in 1515.

Extensions planned at Sheffield Cathedral before the Second World War were completed in the 1960s; this is the modern narthex entrance.

Imaginative designs using modern technology and materials are to be seen at the Roman Catholic cathedrals of Clifton, Liverpool, and, even more recent, Brentwood and Middlesbrough.

And so into the twenty-first century.

A unique enterprise like building a cathedral and keeping it safe and weather-proof – indeed beautiful as well – never really ends and constant maintenance is always a costly challenge because of the special nature of the work and craftsmanship involved. There are, to state the obvious, fewer and fewer craftsmen and women with the skills required for this work. We need to be forever appreciative and grateful for what the few continue to achieve.

GLASS, STONE AND WOOD

THE THREE VISUAL arts that especially come into their own in a cathedral are stained glass and stone and wood carving. Indeed it was the Church, and in particular the great cathedrals and abbeys, which were among the earliest patrons of these arts.

The man in charge of the actual building of a medieval cathedral was the master mason. He was responsible for drawing up plans, choosing stone at the quarry and employing labourers and craftsmen – the stone-masons, the carpenters, the glaziers, the stone-carvers and so on. Each mason identified the stone on which he had been working with his own mason's mark. This helped when his wages were being calculated and also encouraged a high standard of workmanship. Some highly skilled craftsmen were much in demand and they travelled from one place to another. The craftsmen also had their own guilds, not unlike trade unions, and they lived on the building site in lean-to huts called lodges. Once the building of the foundations and main structure was completed numerous craftsmen could start work on the pillars, the roof and the window spaces.

STAINED GLASS

The glaziers had their own craft guilds, of which there were over fifty in York alone. Five to six hundred years ago the making of stained glass, although expensive, was far more widespread than it is today. Colourful windows to beautify a church and tell the story of Christianity to illiterate people were thought a necessity for the House of God, more so even than a good floor! One of the most important centres for making stained glass was York. Some of the windows in the Minster today were made in workshops in Stonegate. One method of producing

Opposite: York Minster: the Five Sisters window (c.1260) in the north transept is the largest and finest medieval *grisaille* (silver-grey glass) window in the world.

Three of the famous 'Miracle Windows' in the Corona, or Becket's Crown, at the east end of Canterbury Cathedral. Dating from 1200, they depict some of the amazing miracles wrought at the martyr Archbishop Thomas Becket's tomb; the accounts of these were compiled long ago by two monks, William and Benedict.

stained glass was to add colour to molten glass. Another way was to brush paint over small fragments and then scratch the design on to them. After reheating the glass to fix the design, the pieces were joined together with lead, very much like a glass jigsaw puzzle! All this was then carefully raised into the window space, where more lead fittings were prepared in the stone supports and transoms. The mid-fourteenth-century tracery of the east window of Carlisle Cathedral is one of the most glorious and beautiful.

York Minster possesses the oldest fragment of stained glass in England, dated *c.*1150. Also in the minster is the famous window called the Five Sisters, now over seven hundred years old. Unlike most stained glass, which is pictorial, the glass in these five lancet windows is covered with abstract patterns in yellows, greens and browns with a greeny-grey background, which is called *grisaille*. This type of glass is especially translucent and these are the finest examples in England. Throughout the minster there are many fine examples of stained glass. They represent more than half of all the precious stained glass in the city of York and this city has more than any other in the whole of Britain. The huge east window was made by the glass painter John Thornton of Coventry at the beginning of the fifteenth century.

At Canterbury are the Miracle Windows, made about 1200. Soon after the murder of Becket some monks wrote a record of the miracles which had taken place at the martyr's tomb. These were translated into stained glass and set up in the windows around the shrine. The cathedral has over

1200 square metres of stained glass and much conservation is carried out in its own special studio.

At Lincoln, the Dean's Eye is a great rose window in the north transept also dating from the beginning of the thirteenth century. Across in the south transept is the Bishop's Eye. Rose windows are symbols of the cosmic and divine; they embody philosophic thought, mathematics and science and are often complex, spectacular and beautiful. They are among the greatest achievements of the cathedral builders.

Dating from about 1350, the great east window at Gloucester is the largest of its kind in Britain and it contains much of its original glass. It is, in a sense, a war memorial to those involved in the French wars of the fourteenth century. Known as the Crecy Window, it was built soon after that battle. It embodies two side pieces at an angle, enabling the use of as much glass as possible.

STONE CARVING

Examples of stone carving, the famous 'Leaves of Southwell' have already been mentioned – a delightful array of foliage which includes ivy, hawthorn, hop, oak and many others, with pigs, lizards, birds and dogs. Of a much earlier date are the Romanesque carvings at Rochester, Ely and Lincoln and in the crypt at Canterbury. Chichester possesses two of the earliest and most famous sculptures depicting Christ. At Wells the capitals of the pillars in the nave and transepts are of the famous stiff-leaf design, unique to England. Some of the carvings tell a story, for example of the fruit stealers and their downfall! Amidst the leaves appear birds, strange creatures and grotesque heads.

One of the many wonderful wood carvings at Chester Cathedral.

WOOD CARVING

Most cathedrals, but notably Chester, Manchester and Ripon, possess some very fine wood carving.

Vibrant colours and vivid design: the high altar tapestry by John Piper in Chichester Cathedral.

Misericords or miserere seats are wonderfully carved on the undersides. These are a form of tip-up seat with a small carved projection, against which the priest or monk could lean for support when standing during the very lengthy services. The subjects of the carvings are greatly varied. Among the Norwich misericords there is a schoolmaster whacking a naughty boy; at Worcester the seasons are represented; Manchester choir stalls include a fox in various situations; at Ripon biblical stories are depicted – Joshua and Caleb carrying grapes, and Jonah and the whale. The Winchester Cathedral choir stalls are among the earliest. These even include a carved face with a moving tongue. At Chester the desk ends are also extremely fine, depicting a Jesse tree, an elephant and castle (also at Ripon) and a delightful little chap with his walking stick. The craftsmen were not limited to what we would acknowledge as 'sacred' subjects and must have enjoyed themselves poking fun at their contemporaries, for the carvings are often full of symbolism and satire.

Exeter has a superb bishop's throne, 60 feet high and most exquisitely carved in the early 1300s. St Paul's Cathedral has superb carving by the Renaissance craftsman Grinling Gibbons. The stalls at Durham, burned for firewood by prisoners in the seventeenth century, were replaced, but the name of the craftsman is not known.

Opposite: The stunning view from the Norman apse of Norwich Cathedral, looking through the choir and crossing, and beyond right to the west window.

Modern artists, craftsmen and craftswomen continue to be commissioned and their work is often of great spiritual intensity. Much of beauty, value and insight will be missed by those who seek only the handiwork of the past.

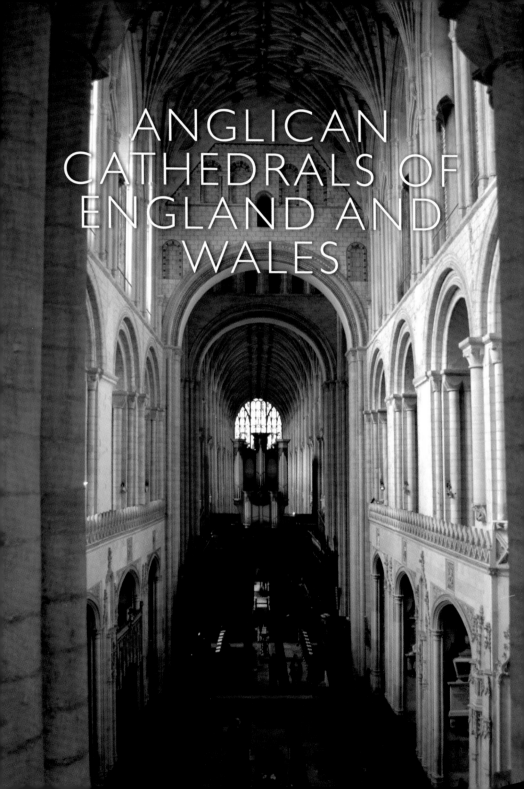

ANGLICAN CATHEDRALS OF ENGLAND AND WALES

BANGOR
CATHEDRAL CHURCH OF ST DEINIOL

The diocese covers the whole of the north-western quarter of Wales, taking in the old counties of Anglesey, Caernarfon, Meirionnydd and the northern portion of Montgomeryshire. Cathedral of ancient origin, the second oldest in Britain after Whithorn.

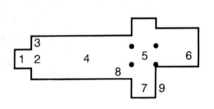

1. Skeffington Tower
2. Wood-carving of the Suffering Christ
3. Site of the consistory court
4. Nave
5. Central tower
6. Sanctuary
7. Lady Chapel
8. Commemorative slab
9. Bricked-up window and buttress

Bangor Cathedral's western tower was completed in 1532.

A MONASTERY WAS founded at Bangor (which means 'wattle fence') in 525 by St Deiniol, who became bishop in 546. The original church here was his cathedral. The fabric has suffered from invaders and native rebels and has undergone frequent repair. There are a few remains of the Norman church; most of the present fabric is of the sixteenth and nineteenth centuries; the last restoration was in the 1960s.

This is a small cruciform building with two towers, right next to the road. The nineteenth-century restoration was very substantial. The main entrance is at the west end (1) and this is also the Skeffington Tower, named after the bishop who built it in 1532. It is embattled and buttressed and has small corner pinnacles. One of the treasures here, carved in oak, is the Suffering Christ (2), called a bound rood and

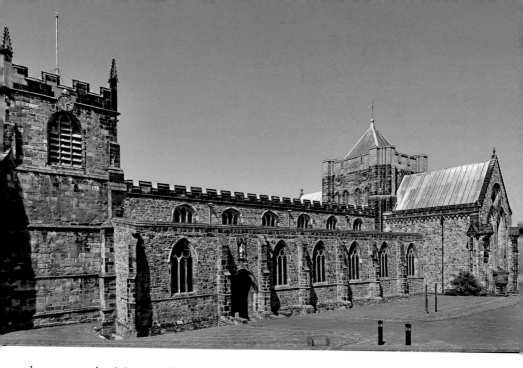

known as the Mostyn Christ after Lord Mostyn, who gave it on permanent loan. The north-west corner was once the site of the consistory court of the diocese (3). The Eva Stone is fourteenth-century. Displayed here are very attractive medieval floor tiles found during the nineteenth-century restoration by Sir George Gilbert Scott. The simple unadorned arcade of the nave (4) leads to the lofty arches at the crossing and the central tower (5) and beyond to the fine east window lighting the high altar and the sanctuary (6). The carved choir stalls date from 1879. The oldest part of the cathedral is in the south wall of the chancel, near the south transept: the bricked-up window and flat buttress are more evident from outside (9). The Lady Chapel (7) is in the south transept; the mural of 'The Journey to Emmaus', showing the disciples in modern dress, is by Brian Thomas. A stone slab in the south aisle (8) commemorates two rulers, Gruffudd ap Cynar (died 1137) and his son Owain Gwynedd (died 1170). There is a simple grandeur here in the heart of this North Wales university city.

Bangor Cathedral: a small cruciform building with a low pinnacle tower, it is the second oldest foundation in Britain.

BIRMINGHAM
CATHEDRAL CHURCH OF ST PHILIP

Diocese: Birmingham, parts of Staffordshire, Warwickshire and Worcestershire.
Became a cathedral in 1905.

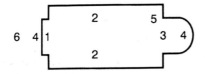

1. West tower
2. Galleries
3. Wrought-iron chancel screen
4. Stained glass windows
5. Organ
6. Statue to Dr Gore

WHEN THIS FINE church was built in the early eighteenth century to a design by the Warwickshire architect Thomas Archer it was at 'the summit of the highest eminence in Birmingham' and very much in the country. Fortunately it is still set in a churchyard fittingly described as the

'lung' of Britain's second city. King George I donated £600 towards the cost of completion in 1725, including the great west tower with its Italian Baroque corner buttresses surmounted by a dome and cupola (1).

The cathedral is still basically the parish church that it was originally and fortunately escaped the heavy bombing endured by the rest of this city in the Second World War. The first British cathedral church which has no direct Gothic elements, it has retained the galleries (2) above the side aisles, typical of the style generally called English Baroque. The cool elegance of the white fluted columns, lightly highlighted in gold, contrasts with the richness of the chancel and its stained glass. The splendid wrought-iron chancel screen (3) was originally the communion rail of the church. When the chancel was extended at the end of the nineteenth century, an important and splendid addition was made, namely the notable Pre-Raphaelite stained glass windows in the chancel and at the west end. These were designed by Sir Edward Burne-Jones, who had been baptised in this church, and made by William Morris (4). Thomas Schwarbrick of Warwick built the organ in 1715; it is considered one of the best early-eighteenth-century organ cases in England (5). In 1765 Jeremiah Clarke, who wrote the Trumpet Voluntary, was the organist here. There is also a memorial to Bishop Leonard Wilson, 'Confessor for the Faith' as a prisoner of war. A statue to Dr Gore, the first Bishop of Birmingham, stands in the churchyard near the west door (6). Close by is an unusual gravestone recording

Opposite:
The statue of Dr Charles Gore (1853–1932), the first Bishop of Birmingham (1905–11).

Thomas Archer's elegant, somewhat Italian Baroque nave of 1715 for what is now Birmingham Cathedral. The central window by Burne-Jones depicts the Ascension.

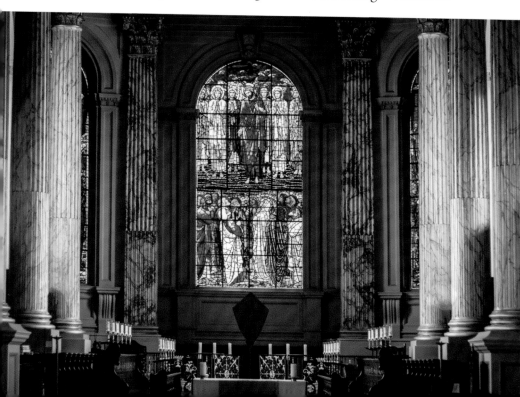

Enjoying the sunshine. The immediate surroundings of St Philip's Cathedral in Birmingham are an oasis of peace in this busy modern city.

the smallest woman who ever lived in Britain, and who was only 33 inches tall.

A memorial, dedicated in November 2004, commemorates the twenty-one people who were killed by IRA bombs at two Birmingham public houses in 1974 – one of Britain's worst terrorist atrocities.

This cathedral is also a parish church and two of its initiatives, 'Believing in Birmingham' and 'Chaplaincy Plus', help promote ecumenical work in the business and commercial community. The 'Justice, Peace and Social Action Group' also meets regularly in the Undercroft and is much involved with refugees and asylum seekers. *Hunger Hut* was installed outside as part of the End Hunger Fast Campaign.

BLACKBURN

CATHEDRAL CHURCH OF ST MARY THE VIRGIN

Diocese: most of the modern county of Lancashire. Became a cathedral in 1926.

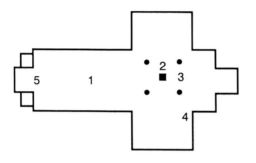

1. Nave
2. High altar
3. Corona
4. Madonna and Child relief
5. Sculpture of Christ the Worker

IT IS HIGHLY probable that there was a Christian church here as early as the sixth century. However, much of the present building of what was formerly the parish church was designed by the architect John Palmer in the Gothic style of the Middle Ages and built in the early nineteenth century. Work in more recent years has made this cathedral an imaginative blend of old and new.

The graceful nave built by John Palmer, a pioneer of the Gothic Revival, has a Gothic roof complete with painted bosses (1). A fire in 1831 necessitated reconstruction. The removal of the galleries in 1964 has made it a beautifully light church. The high altar (2), set in the central crossing below the lovely octagonal lantern, was designed to be seen to great effect from all parts of the cathedral. Over it is suspended a large metal corona (3), suggesting both a crown of thorns and a royal diadem. The complete design forms an impressive entity. The cross on the spire above the lantern contains a commemorative parchment and newspapers for 27th May 1967, the day it was erected. A replica of the fifteenth-century

Madonna and Child relief found in 1820 hidden in a gravestone graces the south transept (4). The last thing seen on leaving the cathedral is the striking sculpture on the west wall of Christ the Worker by John Hayward (5). The shape of its surrounding wrought-iron aureole suggests a loom in a Lancashire weaving shed. There is a regeneration scheme to improve facilities and *Sanctuary: Love never ends* is a youth event through the night with a variety of activities.

The slender spire of Blackburn's elegant lantern tower was completed in 1965.

BRADFORD
CATHEDRAL CHURCH OF ST PETER

Diocese: Since Easter Day 2014 amalgamated with the dioceses of Ripon/Leeds and Wakefield to form the Diocese of West Yorkshire and the Dales. Became a cathedral in 1919.

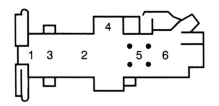

1. Tower
2. Nave
3. Font
4. Balme Memorial
5. Lantern tower
6. Chancel

WOOL AND WEAVING mills have dominated the story of this city; in the nineteenth century it was known as the metropolis of the worsted industry. This fine, late medieval Perpendicular church, a rebuilding in millstone grit on the rising ground of Church Bank, is a most dignified focal point, reflecting the prosperity and confidence of this ancient town and giving no hint of the damage it has suffered from time to time in its history.

From the base of the tower (1), 100 feet high and completed in 1508, there is a good view of the nave (2), just slightly younger, looking east towards the chancel, which was completely rebuilt in 1963. (In the Civil War the outside of the tower was protected from Royalist cannonballs with woolpacks!) The nineteenth-century nave roof has fine coloured roof bosses, angel carvings and masons' marks. There is a remarkable carved medieval font cover (3). In the north transept (4) is the Balme Memorial, perhaps the finest work of the celebrated eighteenth-century sculptor John Flaxman, depicting a bearded gentleman reading to a boy and a girl. A roundel on the east wall recalls the fire at the Bradford

The pinnacled west tower of Bradford Cathedral was built in 1508.

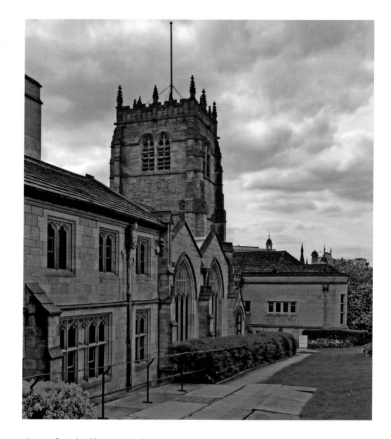

City football ground on 11th May 1985. The west end of the chancel is beneath the lantern tower (5). The chancel (6) is lit partly from the Lady Chapel by splendid stained glass windows, originally in the east window, made in 1863 by the firm of William Morris and designed by Edward Burne-Jones and Dante Gabriel Rossetti. On the canopy of the Provost's stall appears, appropriately, the figure of St Blaise, patron saint of woolcombers – and throat sufferers!

The 'Listening Room' is an unusual feature. The Ministry of Healing is an especially valued strand in this cathedral's life and work. *Difference and Diversity* are being explored in links with the Muslim community under the government's Faith in Action scheme.

BRECON
CATHEDRAL CHURCH OF ST JOHN THE EVANGELIST

Diocese (called Swansea and Brecon): made up of the deaneries of Maelienydd, Builth, Brecon, Hay, Crickhowell, Cwmtawe, Llwchr, Penderi, Swansea, Gower and Clyne. Became a cathedral in 1923.

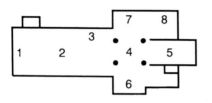

1. Font
2. Nave
3. St Keynes' Chapel of the Corvizors
4. Tower
5. Chancel
6. South transept
7. North transept
8. Havard Chapel

H ERE, BENEATH THE triple peaks of the beautiful Brecon Beacons, the first Norman lord, Bernard de Neufmarche, founded a priory after his victory in 1093 over Rhys ap Tewdwr. It became a parish church at the Reformation. It was known as 'the second cathedral church' of the old diocese

Once a Benedictine Priory, Brecon Cathedral has a pleasant rural setting; its low battlemented tower (1220s) pervades a sense of quiet confidence both inside and out.

The very large medieval cresset stone at Brecon, with thirty cups for holding the oil burnt to provide lighting.

of St David's. It once contained a roodscreen venerated by pilgrims. The massive embattled walls and fine tower are most evocative in this delightful rural setting.

Beneath the fourteenth-century west window stands an ancient font (1) and above this hangs a lovely chandelier of 1772. Nearby is a rare cresset stone, used for oil lighting.

The nave (2) was built early in the fourteenth century in the Decorated style with octagonal pillars, above which are set the clerestory windows; usually they are set above the arches. Wooden screens once separated the side-aisle chapels of four craft guilds. Only one remains, the St Keynes' Chapel of the Corvizors (cordwainers or shoemakers) (3), in the north aisle, separated from the nave by a parclose screen. The fourteenth-century effigy in the ornate recessed alcove is thought to be of the man who supervised the building of the nave.

The choir stalls (1874) are under the tower (4), which was built, together with the chancel and the transepts, in the early thirteenth century in pure Early English style. There are wall paintings on the two western pillars of the tower. The splendid stone-vaulted chancel (5) is simple and elegant with five stepped lancet windows above the lovely stone reredos (1937). The stained glass is dedicated to the memory of the officers and men of the 24th Regiment South Wales Borderers who were killed at Isandhlwana and Rorke's Drift in the Zulu Wars of 1879. There is a rare triple piscina in the south wall of the sanctuary and triple sedilia. The transepts (6, 7) are also lit by tall lancet windows and twin arches lead to restored side chapels, on the south side St Lawrence's Chapel and on the north the Havard Chapel (8). This is now the regimental chapel of the South Wales Borderers and contains memorials and the colours (encased in 2002 to prevent deterioration), including the colour taken by the Zulus at Isandhlwana.

The Heritage Centre in the restored tithe barn provides a fascinating insight into the cathedral's history and aspects of its ministry today. Many cathedrals have residential Choir Schools or the equivalent that young people attend on a daily basis. Brecon Cathedral, however, relies on a faithful and entirely voluntary choir at present. The Cathedral Choir Endowment Appeal seeks to fund and safeguard the all-important choral tradition and to provide subsidized musical education of young choristers in the future. A *2020 Vision Strategy* for the diocese focuses on *Gathering, Growing and Going.*

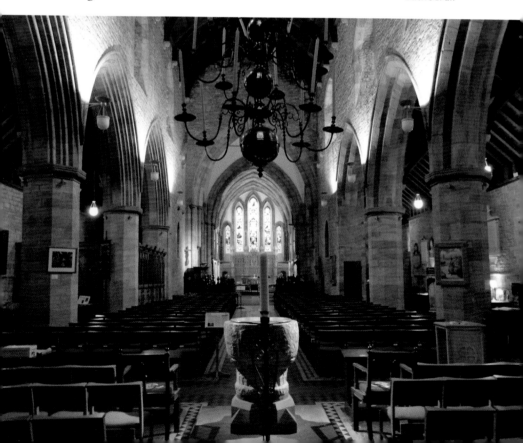

The five Early English lancet windows behind the High Altar stone reredos (1937) in Brecon Cathedral.

BRISTOL
CATHEDRAL CHURCH OF THE HOLY AND UNDIVIDED TRINITY

Diocese: Bristol, small parts of Gloucestershire and Wiltshire. Became a cathedral in 1542.

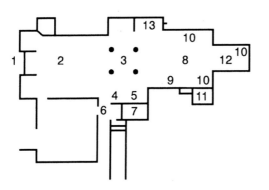

1. West front
2. Nave
3. Central tower
4. 'The Harrowing of Hell' carving
5. Night stair
6. Cloister
7. Chapter house beyond vestibule
8. Choir
9. South choir aisle
10. Star-shaped niches
11. Berkeley Chapel
12. Eastern Lady Chapel
13. Elder Lady Chapel

BRISTOL WAS A celebrated port in medieval times; an Augustinian monastery had been established here in 1140 and there is an ancient tradition that Augustine, the first Archbishop of Canterbury, met other Christians here, where an oak tree once stood. Henry VIII closed the abbey and made it a cathedral when he formed the new diocese of Bristol in 1542. The first women priests in the Church of England were ordained here on 12th March 1994.

From the outside much of what we see today looks like nineteenth-century building and restoration: for example, the west front (1) and the nave itself (2). But in its nineteenth-century work as well as the original medieval building east of the crossing (with England's earliest lierne vault) this is the only example in Britain of a 'hall church', in which the aisles are as tall as the central nave. All this evokes a wonderful feeling of space and of long vistas all around between the pillars.

The second wonder of this church is the lierne vaulting of the choir (8): in about 1300, for the first time in England, the architect not only used the supporting ribs to form a pattern but added decorative ribs (liernes) to create these unusual kite shapes. At the crossing stands the central tower (3), added sometime between 1475 and 1525. The style of vaulting of the choir was repeated here. Set into the east wall of the south transept is a fine late Anglo-Saxon carving of 'The Harrowing of Hell' (4). Nearby is the Norman night stair leading to the monk's dormitory (5). To the south, off the one remaining, fifteenth-century cloister (6), is the beautiful late Norman chapter house, entered through a fine vaulted

An aisle in Bristol Cathedral showing the unique manner in which the vault rests on 'bridges' supported by arches with pierced spandrels.

The fourteenth-century star-shaped recesses contain tombs. This series of stellate niches is unique.

vestibule (7). Roofing the south choir aisle (9) is yet another striking vault, in which the 'bridges' across the arches carry the vault's weight back to the outer walls. Along this aisle and directly ahead are the first of several remarkable 'star'-shaped niches (10). On the right is the sacristy, which has a fascinating and instructive open-ribbed vault. The furthest left of the three niches was once an oven for baking communion bread. Ahead, through a doorway decorated with ammonites, is the delightful Berkeley Chapel (11), with its unique sixteenth-century candelabrum and the loveliest stellate recess for a tomb. The brilliantly coloured Eastern Lady Chapel (12) is dominated by the unusual east window and the great reredos below, which is part of the architectural design; more star-shaped recesses in the walls contain the effigies of former abbots. The Elder Lady Chapel (older by at least fifty years than its neighbour) (13) has intriguing carved

The lower part of the Abbey Gatehouse at Bristol Cathedral is a remarkable survival from Norman times (late 1100s). Notice the characteristic rounded arch with four courses of splendid moulding.

stonework, with animal groups such as monkey and sheep musicians, on which traces of paint can still be seen.

Bristol, once England's second city, has important associations with Methodism. John Wesley's New Room in Broadmead was his headquarters in the west of England. In 2003 both the city and the cathedral, like other parts of the country, commemorated the tercentenary of John Wesley's birth. In the eighteenth century, however, Bishop Butler of Bristol regarded Wesley, an Anglican all his life, with suspicion. He considered his enthusiasm 'a very horrid thing' – a sad reflection on the state of the established church then. However, nowadays, cathedrals have often been at the front line of protest and awareness of political and social issues; in recent years as elsewhere (e.g. St Paul's in London and Sheffield) this cathedral has been challenged by the Occupy Protest Camp movement.

Bristol Cathedral from the north-west, seen across College Green, the ancient precinct of the Augustinian monastery.

CANTERBURY
CATHEDRAL CHURCH OF CHRIST

Diocese: east Kent, east of the river Medway. Founded as a cathedral in 597. The mother church of the Anglican Communion.

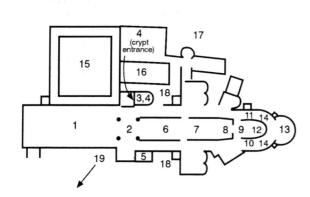

1. Nave
2. 'Bell Harry' tower
3. Site of the martyrdom of Becket
4. Steps to the Norman crypt
5. Warriors' Chapel
6. Choir
7. Presbytery
8. High altar
9. Trinity Chapel – site of shrine
10. Tomb of the Black Prince
11. Tomb of Henry IV and Joan of Navarre
12. St Augustine's Chair
13. Corona
14. Ambulatory
15. Great Cloister
16. Chapter house
17. Water tower
18. Norman towers
19. Christ Church Gate

CANTERBURY'S HISTORY IS closely bound up with the history of England and the lives of famous people. Both the monastery and the cathedral were founded by a mission from Rome in 597; Augustine was the first Archbishop, and the 105th was enthroned in 2013. The bleak tomb of the Black Prince (died 1376) is here (10), as is the splendid alabaster monument of Henry IV (died 1413) and his queen, Joan of Navarre (11). But it was the shrine of Archbishop Thomas Becket (9), murdered in the cathedral on 29th December 1170, that became one of the most visited in Christendom, not least by Chaucer's pilgrims.

The recently restored Great South Window (1420) contains early stained glass dating from 1180. In the Middle Ages stained glass depicting Bible stories taught the Faith to those unable to read; it was the 'poor man's Bible'.

Just beyond the long lofty Perpendicular nave with its fine lierne vault built by Henry Yevele (1, see page 15), and almost at the centre of the cathedral, is the magnificent fan-vaulted lantern of the great 'Bell Harry' tower (2), built at the end of the fifteenth century by John Wastell, who inserted elaborate strainer arches between the piers on three sides to take the

Passing through Christ Church Gate from the Butter Market, the great towers of Canterbury Cathedral 'strike awe into the heart of the beholder', as the scholar Erasmus put it 500 years ago. On the porch recent sculptures of Queen Elizabeth and Prince Philip were dedicated (2015) to commemorate the Royal Jubilee (2012).

extra weight. Just to the north, the site of the martyrdom of Becket (3) is a most evocative place to pause before the stark Altar of the Sword's Point beneath its dramatic sculpture. From here steps descend to the vast Norman crypt (4), with the same layout as the church above. The Chapel of Our Lady of the Undercroft has an altar flanked by fine fourteenth-century screens. In the apse of St Gabriel's Chapel were discovered in 1952 a set of twelfth-century wall paintings. Most notable is the fine Romanesque carving of the columns and their capitals. The Jesus Chapel dedicated to the saints and martyrs of the present time is a poignant reminder of present-day persecution. One emerges in the south-west transept, and immediately on the left is the colourful Warriors' Chapel (5), where Lady Margaret Holland (died 1439) and her two husbands lie and which is full of later memorials.

The Altar of the Sword's Point and its cruciform sculpture are located on the spot in the north-west transept of Canterbury Cathedral where Thomas Becket was slain on 29th December 1170.

Beyond the great stone screen, bearing early-fifteenth-century sculptured figures of kings, rise the choir (6) and the presbytery (7), the first Gothic building in England, begun in 1175 by the Frenchman William of Sens. The Trinity Chapel (9), the site of Becket's shrine, and the Corona (13), completing this superb setting, were built by William the Englishman after William of Sens fell from high scaffolding. The site has been a focus for pilgrims ever since. At the top of the easternmost flight of steps is St Augustine's Chair (12), made from Purbeck marble in the thirteenth century and still used for enthronements. In the choir

aisles and the ambulatory (14) is superb stained glass of the
thirteenth and fourteenth centuries, some of the magnificent
medieval glass throughout the cathedral. Outside to the north
are the vaulted Great Cloister, richly decorated with armorial

Part of the cloisters (normally on the south side) on the north side.

Previous page: The soaring, majestic nave of Canterbury Cathedral, a masterpiece in the early Perpendicular style, looking west from one of the strainer arches or 'stone girders'. These were wisely inserted in the early 1500s when the central tower, England's finest, was built. The west window and some of its glass dates from the early fifteenth century.

Opposite: The beautiful east end of Canterbury Cathedral, the legacy of William of Sens and William the Englishman.

shields (15), the long high chapter house (16), with its superb carved wooden wagon-vaulted ceiling, the splendid water tower (17) and other monastic buildings. Walking around the cathedral on the outside, notice the two superb little Norman towers (18) and Christ Church Gate, through which visitors enter the precinct (19).

1997 was the 1400th anniversary of the momentous mission of Augustine from Rome; it was the inspiration for ecumenical co-operation and endeavour to bring the Christian Gospel afresh to many communities across Europe. There was a pilgrimage from Rome to Canterbury, which fanned out across Britain, to Wales and the north-west, to York, Durham and Lindisfarne in the north-east, and beyond to Iona in the west of Scotland, linking with the Celtic tradition. The *Canterbury Journey* project promotes a wide range of improvements and initiatives to enrich, educate and sustain the world-wide ministry. Links with the Church Urban Fund have been made by the cathedral's launch of the *Together Canterbury* scheme providing support to those tackling poverty and other issues.

CARLISLE

CATHEDRAL CHURCH OF THE HOLY AND UNDIVIDED TRINITY

Diocese: most of Cumbria. Became a cathedral in 1133. Cumbria is one of the first counties to aspire to be ecumenical in developing 'mission communities' in partnership with the Methodist and United Reformed Churches. Maintaining Christian presence in villages in this mainly rural county is at the heart of this; God for All is the key strategy.

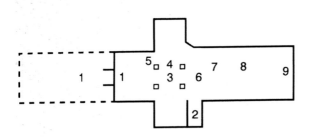

1. Remains of the nave
2. St Catherine's Chapel
3. Tower
4. Perpendicular strainer arch
5. Depressed Norman arch
6. Choir
7. Salkeld Screen
8. Flemish pulpit
9. East window

Carlisle: the Norman south transept and truncated nave (left) seen from the south-west.

L̲ATE IN THE eleventh century a collegiate church was founded here. In 1123 the Augustinians took over and then in 1133 it became the only cathedral in Christendom with an episcopal chapter of Augustinians.

History has not been kind to this cathedral of the Lake District diocese; castle-like in red sandstone, however, it has been described as an oasis of calm and beauty in contrast to the sad and devastating history of this border region. In 1292 a fire which destroyed the town, including the monastery, left the newly built choir a mass of ruins. It also suffered much during the Civil War in the mid seventeenth

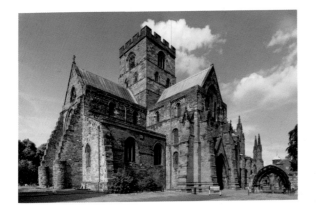

century, when Parliamentary soldiers pulled down part of the Norman nave in order to use the stone to repair the castle and the town walls. The nave was shortened in the nineteenth century to only two bays (1) and Carlisle is unique in having hardly any nave at all! To the right as you enter is St Catherine's Chapel (2), enclosed by the charming sixteenth-century Gondibour Screens. An inscription, *Deo gracias* ('Thanks be to God'), is set into the floor under the tower (3) in thanksgiving for God's blessing through a troubled history. Notice high up the Perpendicular strainer arch to the north (4) and the depressed Norman arch into the south aisle of the short nave (5). Nearby is the entrance to the treasury. In the north transept is the elaborate Brougham Triptych, a splendid early-sixteenth-century altarpiece carved in Antwerp. The choir (6), entered through a fine Renaissance screen, is of great beauty, with splendidly carved pier capitals depicting the months of the year, an ancient painted oak ceiling and fifteenth-century misericord carvings in the stalls; on the backs of the stalls are indications of paintings of the lives of the saints. A notable addition in 1970 was the lovely sixteenth-century Flemish pulpit (8), which complements the Salkeld Screen (7), both on the north side of the presbytery. The remarkable east window (9) is the largest, finest and most richly complex example of curvilinear tracery in England, a true masterpiece and Carlisle's pride.

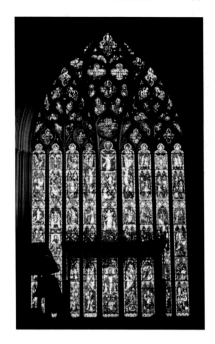

Carlisle Cathedral's pride: the curvilinear tracery of the great east window is exceptionally fine. Rather less than half of the stained glass dates from the fourteenth century, the remainder from the nineteenth century.

In 1653 George Fox, founder of the Society of Friends, the Quakers, preached here. This is the only cathedral in England to have had a complete new ring of bells for the Millennium. *The Fratry Project* in the former dining room of the monks is designed to bring 'untold stories of the cathedral to life' – stories of faith, hope and love – for everyone.

CHELMSFORD
CATHEDRAL CHURCH OF ST MARY THE VIRGIN, ST PETER AND ST CEDD

Diocese: most of Essex, part of Greater London and a tiny part of Cambridgeshire. Became a cathedral in 1914. The book *Coming of Age* tells the story of the hundred years 1914–2014.

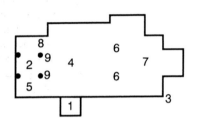

1. South porch
2. Tower
3. Carving of St Peter on buttress
4. Nave
5. St Peter's Chapel
6. Ambos
7. Chancel
8. Bronze relief of 'Christ the Healer'
9. Ancient wall cupboards

IN A TOWN where the world's radio industry was born (at Marconi in Hall Street), this cathedral church has roots far back in the seventh century when St Cedd, the Celtic missionary, established his 'cathedral' at Bradwell-on-Sea. Chelmsford Cathedral has been much enhanced in recent years by extensive reordering, building and furnishing, as befits its role as a mother church of a densely populated diocese. Like several other cathedrals, Chelmsford is, at its core, a late medieval parish church, much altered in the early nineteenth century. The entrance is through a very

The beautiful coved plaster ceiling painted in gentle pastel shades is a replica of the one dating from the 1800s after part of the then parish church collapsed. The nave was rebuilt in the original Perpendicular style but the ceiling was changed.

fine mid-fifteenth-century south porch with characteristic local flint flushwork (1). Of the same period is the impressive buttressed tower (1464), with pinnacles and charming lantern of 1749, surmounted by a needle spire (2). Seated on a buttress at the end of the south choir aisle, St Peter is represented as a modern fisherman complete with waders and a Yale key (3)! In 1990 a new chapter house was opened, described as 'functional with dignity', on a site apart from the main building. The cathedral has Second World War American links.

The most striking feature of the nave (4) is the remarkable coved plaster ceiling painted in pastel shades, a late-nineteenth-century replica of the one built in 1800 after part of the church collapsed. In the south-west corner is the peaceful St Peter's Chapel (5), with an unusual screen and a poignant sculpture, 'The Bombed Child', dedicated to those who suffer. The window depicting St Peter by John Hutton links the cathedral with Bradwell-on-Sea. At the entrance to the chancel (7) note the two modern ambos (lectern/pulpit) with an icon-style cross above each (6). To the left is an unusual fifteenth-century double arch with a central pillar. Beneath the east window is

Opposite: Looking through the unusual fifteenth century double arch with a central fan-like feature to the sanctuary and beyond. Though small compared with most cathedrals, there is a wonderful feel of space, light and intimacy throughout Chelmsford Cathedral.

North of the twin or fan arch at Chelmsford is the monument to Thomas Mildmay, his wife Avice and their fifteen children.

a colourful patchwork of hundreds of crosses, entitled 'Glory', by Beryl Dean. The bishop's chair, by John Skelton, is placed centrally, following ancient tradition. As you retrace your steps to the door, notice near the peaceful St Cedd's Chapel a small wall relief in bronze of 'Christ the Healer' (8). The ancient wall cupboards (9) built into the tower held banners and props used by the town players as late as 1574. In the north transept the 'Tree of Life', painted by Mark Cazalet, celebrates the arrival of Cedd at Bradwell 1350 years ago.

Street Pastors help develop this cathedral's mission in partnership with other denominations in the city and further afield. A Christian resource known as The *God Movie Project* celebrates the goodness of God in creation and daily life.

Although it has humble origins as a medieval parish church, Chelmsford Cathedral exudes a homely dignity and grandeur.

CHESTER

THE CATHEDRAL CHURCH OF CHRIST AND THE BLESSED VIRGIN MARY

Diocese: most of Cheshire, part of Merseyside (the Wirral), tiny parts of North Wales and Derbyshire. Became a cathedral in 1541. On 26 January 2015 in York Minster the Rev Elizabeth 'Libby' Lane, the first female bishop in the Church of England, was consecrated Suffragan Bishop of Stockport in this Diocese of Chester.

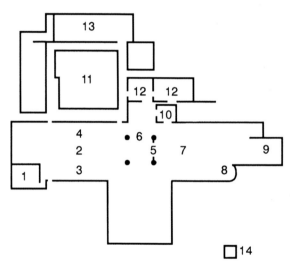

1. Consistory court
2. Nave
3. Grosvenor Westminster Windows
4. Mosaic panels
5. Wooden choir screen
6. Organ case
7. Choir stalls
8. Mosaic panels
9. Lady Chapel
10. Sacristy
11. Cloisters with 'Water of Life' sculpture
12. Vestibule and chapter house
13. Monks' refectory
14. Addleshaw Bell Tower

CHESTER, THE ROMAN garrison town of Deva, is an ancient city with the best-preserved walls in Britain and with reminders of all periods of history since. The cathedral, which is close to the city wall, has suffered much from 'restoration' and also because the red sandstone has decayed. In the tenth century a church was built here and the relics of the saintly Princess Werburgh, an eighth-century nun, daughter of the king of Mercia, were brought here. Anselm, from Bec in Normandy, later Archbishop of Canterbury, came to Chester in 1092 to establish a Benedictine monastery.

Chester
Cathedral from
the Cheshire
Regiment Garden
of Remembrance.
The south
transept (left)
was used as a
parish church
for a time up
to 1881.

For almost 450 years Benedictine monks fulfilled the *opus dei*, the work of God or common worship, and the abbey assumed the form we see today. Then in 1540 the monastery was dissolved but Henry VIII designated it as one of his new cathedrals. The medieval Chester Mystery Plays are still performed. Chester is one of only five cathedrals in England to employ Cathedral Constables.

In the south-west corner of the nave is a rare example of an old consistory court (1636) (1). The nave was begun about 1350 and finished in about 1490 (2). In the south wall are the Grosvenor Westminster Windows, installed in 1992 by Alan Younger in memory of his parents (3). In the north wall (and also in the Chapel of St Erasmus) are nineteenth-century mosaic panels by J. R. Clayton (4, 8). The fine wooden choir screen (5) and the splendid organ case (6) were designed by Sir George Gilbert Scott in 1876. The chief glory of the cathedral, the superb craftsmanship in the woodwork of the choir stalls (7), with their elaborate figure carving, spired canopies, bench ends and misericords, dates from *c.*1390 (see also page 92). Many

fascinating   mythical creatures and characters are represented. The much mutilated base of the early fourteenth-century shrine of St Werburgh stands now near the Lady Chapel (9). In the unusually small north transept is the oldest part of the cathedral, the late   eleventh-century round arch and the arcade above it; through it is the sacristy, formerly a thirteenth-century chapel (10). Just beyond lie the cloisters (11) and the very fine thirteenth-century vestibule and chapter house (12), the

The unusual Addleshaw Bell Tower by George Pace at Chester dates from 1974. The ring is of twelve bells. Compare the medieval bell-tower at Chichester (see page 96).

The nave at Chester looking east towards the choir.

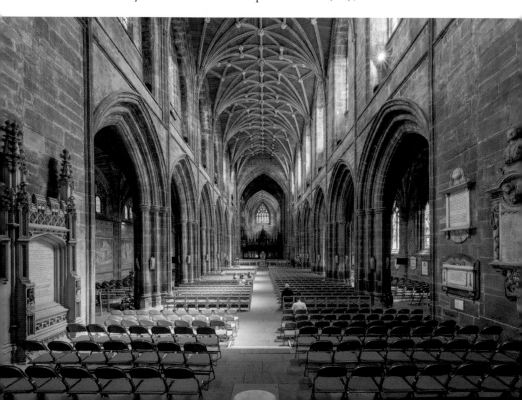

A carved medieval bench end in Chester Cathedral depicting an elephant and castle.

only one of its kind in almost its original form. The monks' refectory or frater is a splendid room with a hammerbeam roof and a rare stone pulpit in the south wall (13), from which a monk would read aloud at mealtimes. This is now the cathedral restaurant, while the purpose-built Song School, completed in 2005, is on the site of the former monks' dormitory. Support for these and 'Sponsor a Pipe' to help restore the famous Grand Organ, are some of the ways to help the cathedral's ministry.

Stephen Broadbent's thought-provoking sculpture 'Water of Life' (1994) in the cloister garden of Chester Cathedral. It depicts Jesus and the woman at the well, recorded in St John's Gospel, chapter 4.

CHICHESTER
CATHEDRAL CHURCH OF THE HOLY TRINITY

Diocese: East and West Sussex and tiny parts of Kent and Surrey. Built as a cathedral in 1070 (the see was at Selsey, 681).

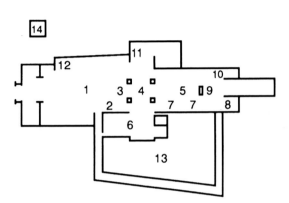

1. Nave
2. Pulpit
3. Bell-Arundel Screen
4. Choir
5. John Piper tapestries
6. South transept
7. Relief carvings of Christ
8. Chapel of St Mary Magdalene
9. Shrine of St Richard
10. Window by Chagall
11. Memorial to Thomas Weelkes
12. Statue of William Huskisson
13. Cloister
14. Bell tower with the statue of St Richard nearby

S T WILFRID, THE 'Star of the Saxon Church' (and much linked with Ripon), began his mission to the South Saxons in 681 at Selsey on the Sussex coast. In 1075 the see was transferred to Chichester and the cathedral was begun here with the broad sweep of the South Downs beyond. Contemporary art is very evident in this cathedral.

Richard of Chichester, 'plain and good like bread', worked tirelessly as bishop for eight years until his death in 1253; his well-known prayer exhorts us to 'see more clearly, follow more nearly and love more dearly'. His shrine was the goal of many a pilgrim. Philip Jackson's statue of the saint stands near the cathedral's west front and the bell tower; it was commissioned for the Millennium.

Although basically Norman, the cathedral is not as grand and overpowering as some others of the period. However, the

Next page: The graceful spire of Chichester Cathedral. Sir George Gilbert Scott's mid-nineteenth-century work replaced the Norman tower and early-fifteenth-century spire which collapsed in 1861.

Philip Jackson's life-size statue of St Richard of Chichester with the tower and spire of the cathedral beyond. St Richard's famous prayer is carved on the plinth of the statue. Peregrine falcons have been nesting in the Central Tower, creating considerable interest.

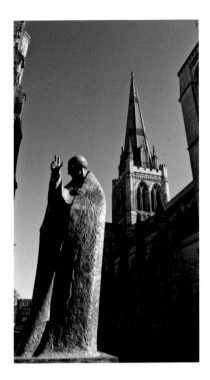

The unique detached medieval bell tower of Chichester Cathedral was completed in 1436. There are eight bells.

nave (1) is surprisingly wide because of the chapels on each side, and there are five aisles. The modern pulpit (2) is by Robert Potter and Geoffrey Clarke. The Bell-Arundel Screen (3) dates from about 1475; restored in 1960, it draws one from the nave towards the choir (4) and beautiful east end, with the glowing colours of the Aubusson tapestries designed by John Piper (5) behind the high altar (see page 60). Paintings in the south transept are by Lambert Bernard, who decorated the main vault, including the Lady Chapel, in the sixteenth century (6). Behind glass in the south choir aisle are two exceptionally fine twelfth-century stone relief carvings of Christ (7). Through a hole in the floor of the aisle can be seen a Roman mosaic of the second century, discovered in 1966. Visible from the far end of the south choir aisle, the painting by Graham Sutherland of Christ appearing to Mary on Easter morning hangs in the chapel of St Mary Magdalene (8). The shrine of St Richard in the lovely retro-choir (9), rebuilt in Early English style after a fire in 1187, attracted many pilgrims until it was destroyed at the Reformation. Marc Chagall designed the colourful window

At Chichester Cathedral the Norman nave begun in 1114 is not as grand as in other cathedrals but the aisles and chapels on each side make it exceptionally wide. The main arcade, triforium and clerestory are clearly seen in this view. The vaulted ceiling was built after a fire in 1187.

The window at Chichester designed by Marc Chagall in 1978 illustrates Psalm 150: 'O, praise God in his holiness...'

The Shrine to St Richard of Chichester in the beautiful retrochoir is backed by the Anglo–German tapestry designed by Ursula Benker-Schirmer and dedicated to St Richard and the local twentieth-century advocate of peace, Bishop George Bell. The Cathedral Restoration and Development Trust founded in 1980 continues to keep as a priority the conservation of the building and its extensive ministry for the benefit of all.

in the north choir aisle (10). The ashes of Gustav Holst are under a slate slab in the north transept, where also, on the west wall, is a memorial to Thomas Weelkes, the great Elizabethan composer (died 1623) (11). At the west end of the north aisle is a statue of William Huskisson MP (12), who in 1830, at the opening of the Liverpool and Manchester Railway, became the first man to be killed by a train. A door in the south aisle leads to a delightful cloister roofed in Irish oak (13). Just north of the west front is the only medieval detached cathedral bell tower in Britain, built in the fifteenth century (14).

COVENTRY
CATHEDRAL CHURCH OF ST MICHAEL

Diocese: most of Warwickshire. A monastic cathedral until the Dissolution. Refounded as a cathedral in 1918. New cathedral, 1962 (old St Michael's destroyed Thursday 14th November 1940). In the Priory Visitor Centre opened in 2001 fragmentary remains of the monastic cathedral can be seen; it was the only medieval cathedral in Britain to have been completely destroyed at the Reformation.

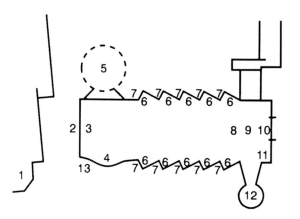

1. Ruins of old church
2. Queen's Steps and porch
3. Glass 'west' wall
4. Baptistery window and font
5. Chapel of Unity
6. Tablets of the Word
7. Stained glass windows
8. Altar
9. Lady Chapel
10. Tapestry of Christ in Glory
11. Chapel of Christ in Gethsemane
12. Chapel of Christ the Servant
13. Sculpture of St Michael and the Devil

IN THE MIDDLE Ages Coventry was a walled town. Lady Godiva was a benefactor of the monastery which was the bishop's cathedral nine hundred years ago. The medieval trade guilds were very influential and they performed miracle or mystery plays which have been revived in modern times (see also Chester, Wakefield, York). The ancient parish church of St Michael was created a cathedral in 1918; its destruction

A symbol of victory over evil. The massive sculpture in bronze of St Michael (patron saint of Coventry Cathedral) defeating the Devil, which was the last great religious work of Sir Jacob Epstein.

The magnificent stained glass Baptistery window on the right is by John Piper while at the far end of the Nave is the large, striking tapestry of Christ in Glory by Graham Sutherland. The cathedral was consecrated on 25 May 1962 in the presence of Queen Elizabeth and her sister Princess Margaret.

on 14th November 1940 gave birth to two inspiring symbols now in the sanctuary of the ruins (1) – the Charred Cross and the Cross of Nails, famous worldwide. The decision to rebuild the cathedral was made the next day. Designed by Sir Basil Spence, who conceived it with great ingenuity and skill, it incorporates familiar elements. The architecture is of the mid twentieth century, employing modern materials and techniques. There is much symbolism in the furnishings and architectural features – old and new concepts, death and resurrection, forgiveness and reconciliation, a journey from Good Friday to Easter.

The ruins are linked to the new building by the Queen's Steps and the porch (2). Straight ahead is the great glass 'west' wall (3) engraved with angels and saints and, in the distance at the far end of the nave, in place of an 'east' window, the striking and dominant tapestry designed by Graham Sutherland of Christ in Glory (10). To the right after entering the cathedral is the brilliant stained glass baptistery window by John Piper and before it is the font, hewn from a boulder brought from Bethlehem (4). On the opposite side is the Chapel of Unity (5), which has tall slender stained glass windows and a beautiful marble mosaic floor. On each side of the nave five shallow, diagonally set V-shaped walls, 70 feet high, punctuate the length: on the sides facing 'west' are the Tablets of the Word (6); on the sides facing 'east' are the majestic stained glass windows (7). The altar (8) is of hammered concrete and in the centre is a beautiful silver-gilt cross symbolising Sacrifice. Behind the altar is a fine screen enclosing the Lady Chapel (9), in which hangs the great tapestry (10). To the right is the Chapel of Christ in Gethsemane (11), screened by a lovely wrought-iron grille by Basil Spence representing the Crown of Thorns. Beyond this is the Chapel of Christ the Servant (12), with clear glass so that the industrial city can be seen. Returning, and leaving by St Michael's Steps, to your left is Epstein's powerful sculpture of St Michael defeating the Devil (13).

A valuable insight at Coventry is in the realm of community and 'the establishment of a creative relationship' in all aspects of life, not least ecumenically and internationally. Coventry is known as a City of Peace and Reconciliation (along with Rotterdam, Warsaw and Dresden). For five years Justin Welby (long before being Archbishop) worked here and led this crucial ministry, helping to heal the widespread hurt after the Second World War.

A symbol of forgiveness and reconciliation. The words 'Father forgive' are carved into the wall behind the Charred Cross in the Sanctuary of the Ruins at Coventry. The cross was formed from two burnt pieces of oak from the roof beams, taken from the blackened ruins after the cathedral was bombed in 1940.

DERBY
CATHEDRAL CHURCH OF ALL SAINTS

Diocese: most of Derbyshire. Became a cathedral in 1927. Extensive refurbishment has taken place and there is a new visitor centre. The cathedral choir has sung evensong in the welcoming Roman Catholic church nearby – an ecumenical first for a cathedral.

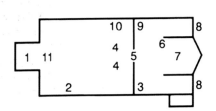

1. Tower
2. South aisle
3. Cavendish Chapel
4. Mayor's pew
5. Wrought-iron screen and gates
6. Bishop's throne
7. Baldachino
8. Coloured windows
9. Old consistory court furniture
10. Portable font
11. Doors to tower

IN THE MIDDLE Ages All Saints, Derby, was a royal collegiate church under the direct care of Lincoln Cathedral. The clerics here lived together as a 'college' and there were monks and nuns round about serving the community. The Trinity Guild, an early trade union, was very prominent here, as indeed were guilds elsewhere. In 1723 the medieval church was so ruinous that the vicar, assisted by hired labourers, is said to have demolished it in one night. Rebuilding followed in the classical Renaissance style although the fine Perpendicular-styled tower (1) remained; it rises to 212 feet. The new church, designed by James Gibbs, was typical of the eighteenth century but the box pews are no longer here. In December 1745 the 'Young Pretender', Prince Charles Edward Stuart, worshipped here on the day he made the fateful decision not to march to London. Sir Ninian Comper planned the changes made when the church became a cathedral; his son Sebastian completed and added to the work.

In the south aisle (2) are some fine monuments by Rysbrack and Sir Francis Chantrey and at the end beyond the screen, in the Cavendish Chapel (3), are the tomb of Bess of Hardwick, who died in 1608, and many other memorials commemorating her descendants. On the south side of the central space (4), in front of the great screen by the fine craftsman Robert Bakewell, is the mayor's pew with magnificent civic ironwork made in 1730, also by Bakewell. Opposite is the County Council pew with modern ironwork designed by Anthony New. The splendid wrought-iron screen and gates (5) across the chancel bear over the gates the arms of the House of Hanover. The bishop's throne (6) is unique for

All that remains of Derby Cathedral's medieval origins is the west tower, one of the largest in the Perpendicular style in England, completed in 1520. The rest of the rebuilding dates from the early eighteenth century (see also page 49).

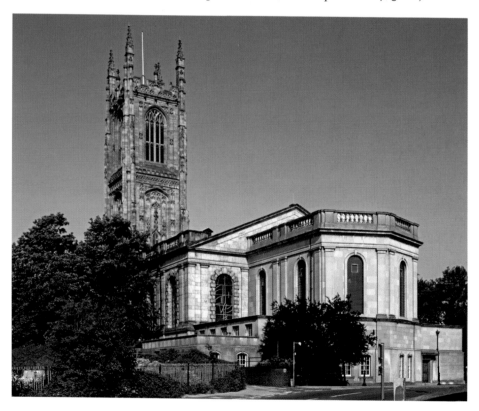

One of a pair of windows in All Saints Cathedral, Derby, designed by Ceri Richards (1965) symbolising 'All Saints and All Souls'.

an English cathedral: it came from a Greek church in Constantinople. In the east walls on either side of the elegant baldachino (7) over the high altar are two coloured windows (8) by the distinguished painter Ceri Richards, installed in 1965. Against the wall of the north aisle stands the furniture of the old consistory court of 1634 (9), which administered church business. On the other side of the screen in front of the pews is the portable font (10) made by Rolls-Royce to a design selected from those submitted as a special project by a group of the company's undergraduate apprentices. Glass doors lead into the tower (11), which contains some of the oldest bells in Britain.

Opposite the cathedral an eighteenth-century listed building is now the Cathedral Centre, comprising a treasury, library and listening room in addition to the usual facilities for visitors. There is also an imaginative garden based on Christian symbols and the concept of pilgrimage.

The Chapel of St Mary on the Bridge, a short distance away from the cathedral, is used regularly as a 'detached' Lady Chapel; most cathedrals have one in the main building. Since 2006 the cathedral has enjoyed the rare publicity nationwide for having peregrine falcons nesting in the tower. The Peregrine Project with its web cameras monitors and updates all the action. The cathedral works with the local Quad Arts' initiative and is also involved with the Annual Well Dressing Festival for which Derbyshire is famous.

DURHAM

CATHEDRAL CHURCH OF CHRIST, BLESSED MARY THE VIRGIN AND ST CUTHBERT

Diocese: most of County Durham, parts of South Tyneside and Teesside. Founded as a cathedral about 997, though the diocese dates from 635.

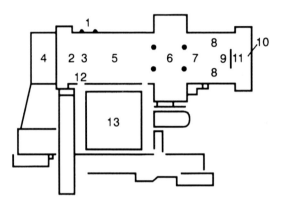

1. 'Sanctuary' door knocker
2. Bishop Cosin's font
3. Black marble line
4. Galilee Chapel – Bede's tomb
5. Nave
6. Central tower and crossing
7. Choir
8. Choir stalls
9. Neville Screen
10. Chapel of the Nine Altars
11. St Cuthbert's tomb
12. Monks' door
13. Cloisters

BEARING THE BODY of Cuthbert, who had died in 687, monks from the Holy Island of Lindisfarne, off the wild Northumberland coast, came at last in 995 to this wooded hill above the loop of the river Wear. They built a shelter, then later a church known as the White Church, to house the saint's body. Work was started on this magnificent cathedral in 1093 and by 1133 what is probably the finest Romanesque church in Europe was complete in most essentials. The Galilee Chapel (4) at the west end, added in 1170–5, was the last phase of the Norman work and the Chapel of the Nine Altars at the east end, finished about 1280, is Early English. There are three imposing towers dominating this World Heritage site.

On the north door is a replica of the splendid twelfth-century lion's head 'Sanctuary' door knocker (1). Straight ahead are Bishop Cosin's font and cover (2), carved in 1663, 40 feet high and gorgeously decorated. Just in front of the font is a black marble line (3). In monastic times women were not allowed east of this point. This is perhaps why the Galilee Chapel (4), which serves as a Lady Chapel, was placed, very unusually, at the west end. In 1370 the remains of the Venerable Bede, the Father of English History and Learning, who had died in 735, were removed here from St Cuthbert's tomb, where they had been since 1022; the black-topped tomb chest which now holds them was installed in 1542. There are splendid twelfth-century wall paintings of St Cuthbert and St Oswald. The superb nave (5) is flanked by massive piers, alternately round and wonderfully incised with geometric patterns or formed by clusters of pillars. These piers, the rib-vaulting of the roofs, which in the transepts is the earliest in Europe, and the magnificent arches and arcades above are the glories of Durham. At the crossing the great arches and fine rib-vaulting of the central tower (6) still convey tremendous Norman strength and confidence. In the choir (7) are the spectacular early

The thick pillars of the Norman Romanesque nave in Durham Cathedral, with their alternating incised patterns in the stonework.

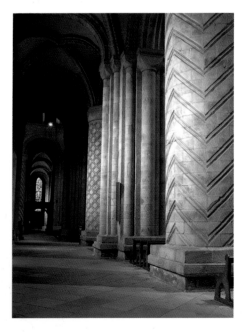

fourteenth-century bishop's throne, ornamentally detailed stalls of 1665 (8) and the high altar, backed by the beautiful Neville Screen (c. 1380) (9). Beyond lies the Chapel of the Nine Altars (10) with tall lancet windows beneath the rose window. Pilgrims gathered here before visiting the shrine of St Cuthbert up the steps (11). Today's pilgrims pray at a simple grey slab of stone which bears the word CUTHBERTUS; here he was finally enshrined in 1104. The statue nearby shows him holding the head of St Oswald, which was originally buried with him. To the south again, through the monks' door with its superb carving and ironwork (12), are the cloisters (13), the monks' dormitory and the treasury, where ancient manuscripts and precious objects are displayed. Durham Cathedral was voted one of Britain's finest buildings. Local heritage and culture are marked by such events as the Durham Miners' Gala Day. *Spiritus*, an initiative led by the bishop, has met on the roof of the central tower for prayer, interceding for the world. The 'Open Treasure Appeal' furthers archaeological research and various projects.

The Romanesque Galilee Chapel (1175) at Durham, which probably marks the last stage of the Sunday Great Procession long ago. Here this is also the Lady Chapel, which is unusual at the west end.

While the west towers are the best known feature of Durham, the view from the east is also most impressive.

ELY

CATHEDRAL CHURCH OF THE HOLY AND UNDIVIDED TRINITY AND ST ETHELDREDA

Diocese: most of Cambridgeshire, small parts of Bedfordshire, Essex, Norfolk and Peterborough. Became a cathedral in 1109.

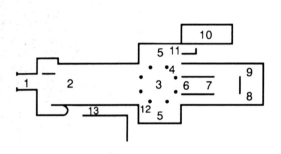

1. Galilee porch
2. Nave and painted wooden ceiling
3. Octagon and lantern tower
4. Eight pillars of the Octagon
5. Transepts
6. Choir
7. Presbytery
8. Chantry chapel
9. Chantry chapel
10. Lady Chapel
11. Stained Glass Museum above in triforium
12. Monks' door
13. Prior's door

THE SIGHT OF this great East Anglian church rising above the flat expanse of the Fenlands is one of the most memorable in Britain. To this remote refuge in 673 came a thirty-three-year-old princess, Etheldreda, to found a double monastery of both monks and nuns; she was installed by her friend St Wilfrid, Archbishop of York. Four hundred or so years later Hereward the Wake made his famous stand against the Normans here. The Puritan Oliver

The Prior's door (c.1140) at Ely, unlike the monks' door, has an elaborately carved tympanum above it, depicting Christ in Majesty, with angels in strange poses.

Previous page: Looking up at the amazing Octagon and Lantern Tower. This, the only Gothic dome (1323–36), is a medieval tour de force in stone, wood and lead. John of Burwell, a local carver, earned two shillings and meals at the prior's table for his carving of 'Christ raising his hand in blessing' in the centre at the top of the Lantern.

Ely's Norman west front had a single tower, unique in Britain. It was later completed with an upper section flanked by corner turrets. It had a wooden spire until 1806. In the floor of this tower is a rare and intriguing unicursal maze; the distance from the start to the centre is the same as the height of the tower.

Cromwell lived locally and later, when in power, was able to ban services for ten years!

At the age of eighty-six Abbot Simeon began the present building in 1083 and most of it was complete by 1189. There were several important alterations and additions to come, such as the lovely Galilee porch (of about 1215) (1), through which we enter the cathedral, a fine example of the Early English style. The nave (2) with its wooden ceiling, painted in the nineteenth century, is exceptionally long and impressive, leading the eye eastwards to the great space beneath the awe-inspiring Octagon and lantern tower (3); this replaced the original Norman tower, which collapsed in February 1322. The total weight of wood and lead is 400 tons. It is a unique medieval masterpiece of engineering and ingenuity, the only Gothic 'dome', a tour de force of the carpenter's skill and that of the designer, Alan of Walsingham, monk and sacrist – his sculptured head may be seen along with stone corbels illustrating St Etheldreda's life

below the niches on the eight pillars of the Octagon (4). Angels support the hammer beams of the highly decorated fifteenth-century ceilings over the transepts (5). Through Sir George Gilbert Scott's screen is the choir (6), also a casualty of the collapse of the tower and beautifully restored in the Decorated style with lierne vaulting and carved bosses. It is separated by single Norman pillars from the magnificent Early English presbytery (7), built to house the shrine of St Etheldreda in 1252 (now marked by a slate tablet). The superb misericords of the fourteenth-century choir stalls are complemented by figure carving on the canopies by nineteenth-century Belgian craftsmen. Where the first and second arches meet above the south choir stalls look for the Ely Imps. There are some ornate tombs and chapels: on either side of the great east window are beautiful chantry chapels of 1533 and 1488 (8, 9). The Lady Chapel (see page 35), unusually placed at the

north-east corner, has one of the widest medieval vaults in England and, despite terrible damage at the Reformation, is still a beautiful building (10). Also in this corner is the entrance to the Stained Glass Museum (11), which is well worth a visit. To see what is left of the cloister, return to the south aisle and go through the highly ornamental monks' door (12). Do not miss the prior's door (13); it is a wonderful example of Norman carving. A stroll round the outside of the cathedral to study the exterior and the monastic buildings and ruins is most rewarding, with many superb vistas. Tours of the Octagon and West Tower give an added, unparalleled dimension to one's experience of this beautiful little city and its cathedral.

The ceiling of the extremely long and lofty nave at Ely was always of wood. It was painted, without fee, in 1858–65.

EXETER
CATHEDRAL CHURCH OF ST PETER

Diocese: Devon, small parts of Dorset and Cornwall. Became a cathedral about 1050 (the see was at Crediton from 909). This cathedral with the western dioceses participates in Carbonfest, playing a part in carbon emission reduction.

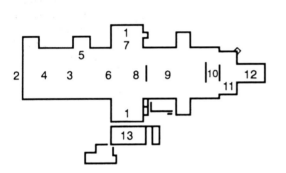

1. Transept towers
2. West front
3. 'Palm' vaulting
4. Becket Boss
5. Minstrels' gallery
6. Tumbler Corbel
7. Ancient clock
8. Great Screen or pulpitum
9. Bishop's throne
10. 'Exeter Pillar'
11. Tomb of Bishop Bronescombe
12. Lady Chapel
13. Chapter house

IN 1003 THE Anglo-Saxon minster was destroyed by Viking pirates but King Canute rebuilt it. Bishop Leofric, whom Edward the Confessor allowed to transfer the seat of the bishopric of Devon and Cornwall here from Crediton in 1050, left his collection of books to the cathedral; among them is the wonderful *Exeter Book*, a collection of Anglo-Saxon poetry.

This cathedral epitomises the peak of the Decorated Gothic style in England; it is a building of remarkable beauty and symmetry, splendidly restored after the bomb damage of 1942. The imposing twin towers at the transepts (1), a very unusual arrangement in

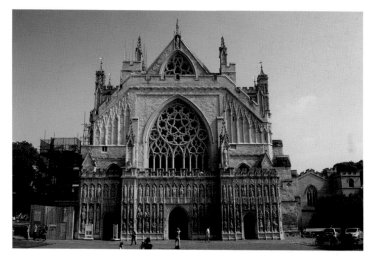

Fine stone carving and sculpture on the west front at Exeter. The stone screen was the last important addition to the cathedral (1370–94). Most of the statues are originals – saints, kings, knights and angels.

England, are almost all that remain of the Norman building. We enter through the sculptured image screen, which forms the lower part of the west front (2). Most of the church we see today was built in the hundred years before 1369. One of Exeter's glories is the continuous stone-ribbed vaulted ceiling and roof 300 feet long (3), the longest and probably finest Gothic vista in the world, with its magnificent 'palm' vaulting, pillars of slender clustered shafts and one of the finest collections of painted roof bosses. Look for the Becket Boss (4), showing his murder, in the nave roof two bays from the entrance, and the Tumbler Corbel at the top of the pillar just beyond the nave pulpit (6). Halfway down the nave, over the north porch, is an unusual minstrels' gallery of c.1350 delightfully carved with an angelic 'band' (5). The clock in the north transept dates from the fifteenth century although the dial is of 1760 (7). Above the superb great screen or pulpitum of 1325 (8) is the organ, its case made by John Loosemore in 1665. The finest medieval craftsmanship went into the bishop's throne (9), 60 feet high, dating from 1312, and the misericords under the stall seats, which are the oldest complete set in England. The stalls are nineteenth-century,

Opposite: The splendid transept towers are almost all that remains of the Norman building at Exeter; they are unique in Britain. A nearby statue of a seated figure commemorates Richard Hooker, an influential sixteenth-century Anglican priest and theologian, born locally, who wrote in support of the reformed English church.

by Sir George Gilbert Scott. Behind the high altar rises the 'Exeter Pillar' of sixteen shafts (10), the first in this lovely style around the cathedral. To the right are exquisitely carved sedilia, seats for the clergy. The magnificent east window above has fourteenth-century glass. The fine tomb of Bishop Bronescombe (11), who began the transformation of the cathedral in 1258, is next to the Lady Chapel (12). The wooden roof of the chapter house is delicately painted to imitate fan-vaults (13). Outside, the pleasant lawned close evokes the intimacy of the whole cathedral.

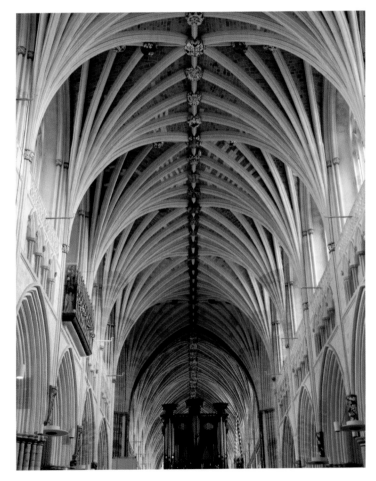

Exuberance in stone at Exeter – the palm-branch effect of the nave roof and beyond, unbroken by a central tower (usual elsewhere). There is 300 feet of tierceron stone-ribbed vaulting (1280s), its length a stunning feature unique to this cathedral.

GLOUCESTER

CATHEDRAL CHURCH OF THE HOLY AND INDIVISIBLE TRINITY

Diocese: most of Gloucestershire, small parts of Oxfordshire, Warwickshire, Wiltshire and Worcestershire. Became a cathedral in 1541.

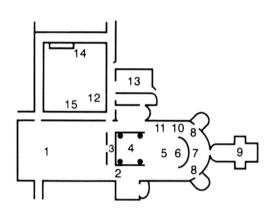

1. Nave
2. Entrance to south transept
3. Organ case
4. Choir
5. Effigy of Robert, Duke of Normandy
6. Heavenly orchestra of angels
7. Crécy window
8. Norman ambulatory
9. Lady Chapel
10. Prisoner of war cross
11. Tomb of Edward II
12. Cloister – earliest fan tracery
13. Chapter house
14. Monks' lavatorium
15. South walk

A SAXON ABBEY at Gloucester was founded in 681 and there was a third monastery on this site when in 1089 the Normans began their great church here, including a crypt which survives (entered from the south transept). King Edward II was ignobly murdered in 1327 at Berkeley Castle, about 20 miles south-west of Gloucester. The Abbot arranged an elaborate burial service here, attended by the royal family. Rather astonishingly, pilgrims came in vast numbers to venerate such an unworthy monarch but the monks did not complain since the revenue this brought in enabled them to begin the transformation of their rather sombre Norman building, a process that continued for 150 years. The Perpendicular Gothic style is very much an invention of the English, their awe-inspiring contribution to later medieval architecture:

At Gloucester Cathedral the corner turrets echo the beautiful central tower itself. Built in the mid-fifteenth century, it is a superb tower of the Perpendicular period, of which Gloucester's east end is a prime example.

Gloucester Cathedral is one of the finest examples. The grace and majesty of the tower are unequalled. The Norman crypt (*c.* 1080) beneath the eastern part of the cathedral had to be reinforced when the vast and revolutionary new Choir was built above in the 1350s.

The nave (1) retains the massive cylindrical Norman piers and the simple arcade, which contrast with the thirteenth-century Early English ribbed vault above. The transformation to Perpendicular style, the earliest still surviving, begins at the entrance to the south transept (2) and is seen in its splendour in the choir (4), where slender columns soar upwards to the lofty lierne vault in front of one of the noblest and largest windows in the world (7). This window commemorates the fallen at the battle of Crecy (1346). An intriguing lower roundel in the stained glass depicts a golfer! The splendid organ case above the screen dates from 1660 (3). East of the fourteenth-century choir stalls, with fine misericords, the thirteenth-century effigy (5) of Robert, eldest son of the Conqueror, lies before the high altar; above is the heavenly orchestra of gilded angels with their instruments (6). On the other side of the Norman ambulatory (8), which runs round the choir, is the charming Lady Chapel (9), once called a 'palace of glass', approached under the 'Whispering Gallery'. In the north ambulatory is the pinnacled tomb of Edward II (11), whose alabaster effigy is one of the finest of its time. Nearby stands the cross (10) carved by Colonel Carne

VC while he was a prisoner of war in Korea. Through doors in the north aisle are the cloister (12) and the Norman chapter house (13), where William I commissioned the Domesday survey at Christmas 1085. The cloister vault is the earliest fan tracery of its kind; it is at its finest, in miniature, in the monks' lavatorium (14). The scriptorium, where the monks each had a study cell, is in the south walk (15). The Three Choirs Festival

Gloucester: the late-fourteenth-century fan-vaulting in the beautiful cloisters is the earliest surviving in England. In the south walk, known as the scriptorium, the monks would study and work, each in his own cubicle or carrel ranged along the side.

The tomb of Edward II in Gloucester Cathedral. The young king Edward III, in his teens, ordered this to be made in memory of his murdered father.

Previous page: The light yet stately atmosphere in the east end of Gloucester Cathedral stands testament to the principles of Perpendicular architecture.

is held at Gloucester in rotation with Hereford and Worcester, every third year. Gloucester Cathedral has been used as a location for many films.

On the north side of the cathedral by the ancient Infirmary Arches is the Herb Garden, a delight to all who have time to enjoy the themed beds of culinary, medicinal and cosmetic herbs. Stone carving also has a high profile here with master mason for over twenty years, French born Pascal Mychalysin. Exhibitions of sculpture entitled 'Crucible' attract thousands of visitors. 'Project Pilgrim – The Heart of Gloucester' aims to tell the story of the people of the cathedral, city and diocese, highlighting conservation and heritage.

The effigy of Robert, Duke of Normandy (died 1134), was made in the thirteenth century. The sarcophagus is later.

GUILDFORD

CATHEDRAL CHURCH OF THE HOLY SPIRIT

Diocese: west Surrey and part of Hampshire. The new diocese was formed in 1927.

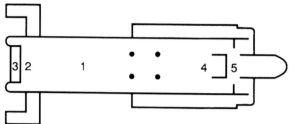

1. Nave
2. Engravings on glass
3. Glazed door
4. Sanctuary
5. Foundation stone

I N 1961 THIS cathedral was described as 'a people's church, built by the people to be used by the people', a reference in part to those who bought and signed the bricks of which it is built. It stands in a prominent position on an ideal site, Stag Hill, and its foundation stone was laid in 1936, nine years after the diocese had been formed out of that of Winchester and four years after Edward Maufe had won the competition

The architect of Guildford Cathedral, Edward Maufe, conceived seven simple arches on each side to lead us forward in spirit. Surrey University usually holds its graduation ceremony in the cathedral.

to design it. It was the first cathedral church to be built on a new site in the south of England since the Reformation. Work was stopped by the Second World War but resumed in the 1950s and the Bishop later described the project as a venture of faith at a time of serious economic difficulties. As part of the cathedrals Golden Jubilee and of the Royal Jubilee Progress, the Queen visited the cathedral in November 2012, fifty years after its consecration, which she had also attended.

As one approaches (probably by car – it has been dubbed the motorist's cathedral), the vista of the west front and majestic central tower surmounted by a golden angel is particularly impressive. The garth-porches to the north and south of the west front both welcome and enfold as a Mother Church should do. The view at the east end, of the apse of the Lady Chapel surmounted by statues of the Archangel Gabriel and

Engraved in the glass of the doors of the west front of Guildford Cathedral are angel musicians by John Hutton. Nine carvings in stone over the doors bring the cathedral's completion a little nearer.

four saints, is equally striking. Here is the Garden of Remembrance dedicated in 1997; nearby is the teak cross made from timbers of HMS *Ganges*.

When one enters, there is an uninterrupted view to the high altar as 'seven simple arches on each side lead us forward in spirit' (1). The style is a soothing, flowing Gothic, very English and understated. It is elegant, light and spacious with touches of colour against muted, peaceful backgrounds. Tall, narrow, deep windows form shadows in the high white-plastered walls. The nave piers are narrow, the aisles lofty. Restful pale paving leads up to the sanctuary. There are furnishings which recall the medieval heritage: the engravings on glass (2), by John Hutton; the blue embroidered kneelers; various modern furnishings and craftsmanship in wood, stone and glass; the sanctuary carpet designed by the architect (4), and not least the ancient stones from Canterbury and Winchester Cathedrals on which the foundation stone rests (5). This is the only cathedral in Britain dedicated to the Holy Spirit: the words *Veni Creator Spiritus* appear above the glazed door (3).

The central sculpture above the west front doors is the Transfigured Christ, thought to be the only one in existence. In keeping with the cathedral's dedication to the Holy Spirit, on either side Charlie Gurrey, the sculptor, chose to portray men and women whose lives 'reflected the Holy Spirit'. The 'Make Your Mark' campaign, like the 'Buy a Brick' project in the 1950s, ensures donors and supporters are still very much part of this 'People's Cathedral' today.

The Lady Chapel at the far eastern end of Guildford Cathedral was consecrated in 1964. The carving by Douglas Stephen of the Madonna and Child was crafted from one trunk of a rare South American hardwood tree. Near the chapel entrance is the cathedral's Foundation Stone.

HEREFORD

CATHEDRAL CHURCH OF THE BLESSED VIRGIN MARY AND ST ETHELBERT

Diocese: Herefordshire, parts of Shropshire and Wales (Welsh Marches), a few parishes in Staffordshire. Founded as a cathedral in 676.

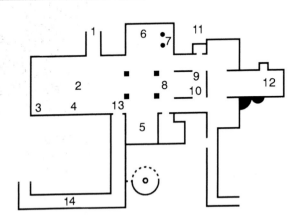

1. North or Booth Porch
2. Nave
3. Norman font
4. Croft Pulpit
5. South transept
6. North transept
7. Bishop Cantelupe's Shrine
8. Bishop's throne
9. King Stephen's chair
10. Statue of Ethelbert
11. Stanbury Chantry Chapel
12. Lady Chapel
13. Door to Bishop's Cloister
14. New Library Building

THERE HAS BEEN a place of worship here on the bank of the beautiful river Wye since the seventh century, when Putta, the first Bishop, a refugee from his sacked cathedral at Rochester, was appointed. He is remembered because he taught his priests and the people to sing and began a musical tradition which some see as continuing today in the Three Choirs Festival (with Gloucester and Worcester). When in 792 the young King Ethelbert of East Anglia was murdered by order of King Offa of Mercia, he was buried here as a martyr and is a patron saint of the cathedral. Another notable figure, Thomas Cantelupe (7), is also commemorated here.

The superb lantern and tower, pinnacled and lavishly decorated with ballflowers, were paid for by the offerings of pilgrims to the shrine of St Thomas Cantelupe, Lord High

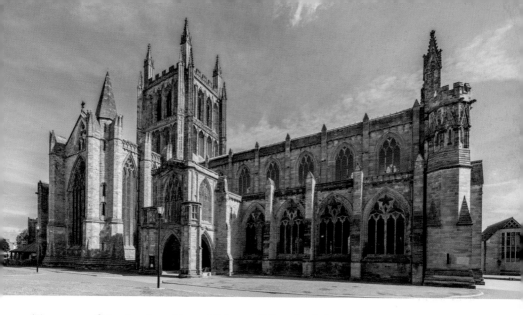

Treasurer of England and later Bishop of Hereford from 1275 to 1282. The cathedral entrance is on the north side, through the beautiful two-storey porch (1) with a sixteenth-century chapel above. Upon entering, one is first aware of the Norman features: the great piers of the nave (2), with their unusual decorated capitals and arches of 1145. In the south aisle there is a fine Norman font (3) and nearby the simple wooden pulpit from which Dean Croft in 1646 bravely admonished the Roundheads for despoiling the cathedral (4). The south transept Norman wall (where now hang three John Piper tapestries) shows what the church must have looked like (5) but the north transept (6) is a great surprise with its almost triangular pointed arches built in the Gothic Decorated style of the late thirteenth century. The Cantelupe Shrine stands here (7). The choir stalls were made in 1375, at the same time as the magnificent bishop's throne (8), which has two seats for chaplains. On the left of the elaborate high altar and reredos by Cottingham is the chair said to have been used by King Stephen in 1138 (9) and to the right is a statue of Ethelbert, the martyred king (10). Just off the north choir aisle is the lovely Stanbury Chantry Chapel (11). At the far east end is the Lady Chapel (12), completed in 1220 and considered one of the

Until 1790 the richly decorated central tower of Hereford Cathedral had a spire. The West Front, not in view on the right, dates from 1908; this replaced the original one destroyed in 1786 when the medieval west tower collapsed. In the close is an unusual statue of Edward Elgar with his bicycle. He lived in Hereford in 1904–11.

Hereford Cathedral has been called 'the ghost of a Norman cathedral' – there have been so many changes and much restoration over the years. The mouldings (see also page 24) on capital and arch, though late Norman, are a very decorative feature. Some critics say that the meeting point of each pillar and arch is not aesthetically pleasing.

most beautiful of its time. The crypt below is reserved for quiet prayer. The door in the south aisle (13) leads to the Bishop's Cloister. The famous Map of the World – 'Mappa Mundi' – and the Chained Library are housed in the New Library Building

The Shrine of St Thomas Cantelupe, Bishop of Hereford 1275–82. The stunning canopy design by Peter Murphy shows saints with the Christ Child (the Light of the World) being presented, appropriately, with 'Mappa Mundi' – the 'world map'.

at the opposite corner of the cloisters (14). Since the Queen opened it in May 1996, it has received worldwide acclaim. The 'Close Connections' project has also been most successful through its wide-ranging activities and initiatives for the benefit of the communities of cathedral, city and diocese.

LEICESTER
CATHEDRAL CHURCH OF ST MARTIN

Diocese: most of Leicestershire, one parish in Northamptonshire. Became a cathedral in 1927 (the diocese is very ancient).

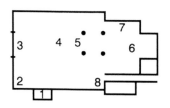

1. Vaughan Porch
2. Chapel of the Royal Anglian/ Leicester Regiment
3. Choir gallery
4. Nave
5. Chancel screen
6. Tomb of Richard III
7. St Katharine's Chapel
8. South aisle

T HE FIRST DIOCESE of Leicester was created in 680 but did not survive the turmoil of the Danish invasions (*c.*870), so there was probably a church on this site in Saxon times – and before that there was a Roman temple. Leicester continued to be an important town throughout the Middle Ages, with a castle, abbey and churches. This outwardly Victorian building is, therefore, an ancient civic church, built and rebuilt and faithfully restored over the past seven hundred years.

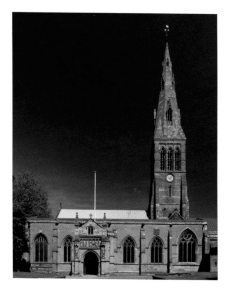

The nineteenth-century tower of Leicester Cathedral is 220 feet high, including the unusual broach spire. One of the finest late medieval parish churches with a blend of styles from the Middle Ages to Victorian, since March 2015 it has been the final resting place of King Richard III.

There are survivals from at least as early as the thirteenth century and interesting memorials to local citizens.

The fine tower and broach spire 220 feet high were rebuilt in the 1860s. The cathedral is entered through the Vaughan Porch (1), built in memory of a nineteenth-century vicar. Just to the left is the regimental chapel of the Royal Anglian/Leicester Regiment (2). Just outside this chapel, in the west wall, a window depicts St Martin, the cathedral's patron (also featured in the east window). The choir gallery with the organ

Members of the Herrick family are commemorated in St Katherine's Chapel, Leicester Cathedral. This window is in memory of Robert Herrick, the priest and poet.

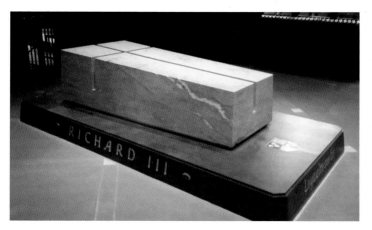

Since March 2015, this modern tomb has housed the remains of the last Medieval king, Richard III. He was the last English king to die in battle.

(parts of which date to 1774) is at the west end (3). Over the high nave (4), the arcades of which date from the mid thirteenth century, is a splendid hammerbeam roof of red pine with painted angels. Where the fine modern chancel screen (5) is now, a rood or cross stood in the Middle Ages, hence the name St Cross as well as St Martin. After some controversy the body of King Richard III was reburied here on 26 March 2015. He was killed in1485 at the Battle of Bosworth and buried near this church in Grey Friars churchyard. His tomb, (6) expresses 'from death into resurrection' and stands between the Chapel of Christ the King and the Sanctuary. The stained glass east window, high altar and reredos are worthy First World War memorials. The poet Robert Herrick is commemorated in the window of St Katharine's Chapel (7), where there are other family memorials. The Great South Aisle (8), added about 600 years ago, was once the Lady Chapel dedicated to Mary the Mother of Jesus. In recent years there has been considerable reordering and changes throughout the cathedral, especially to accommodate the tomb of King Richard III. The cathedral's ministry has also developed and extended near and far. The Workplace Chaplaincy, one of many outreach projects, provides a listening ear and support for all who are anxious and seeking help.

Previous page, top: There has been considerable refurbishment at Leicester Cathedral but the fine proportions and typical features of this notable former parish church remain and serve well as a cathedral. The splendid hammer-beam roof of red pine, with painted angels, was completely renovated in the late1860s.

LICHFIELD

CATHEDRAL CHURCH OF THE BLESSED VIRGIN MARY AND ST CHAD

Diocese: most of Staffordshire; small parts of Shropshire and Warwickshire. Original cathedral foundation c.700 (Mercia, 656). The Two Saints Way, a pilgrimage route of 92 miles, links Chester and Lichfield.

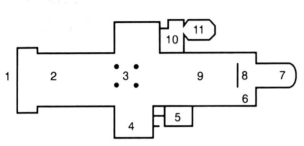

1. West front and spires
2. Nave
3. Choir screen
4. South transept
5. Chapel of St Chad's Head
6. Sleeping Children Monument
7. Lady Chapel
8. Site of shrine of St Chad
9. Minton floor tiles
10. Vestibule
11. Chapter house

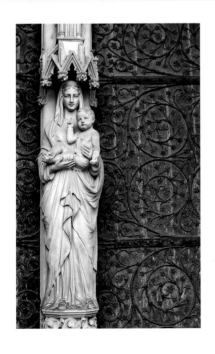

ABOUT 1300 YEARS ago St Chad was baptising people at Stowe Pool near Lichfield in the ancient kingdom of Mercia. After his death in his little chapel on 2nd March 672 his body was long venerated by pilgrims to the stone cathedral which was eventually built here. A Norman cathedral built later was rebuilt in the Early English Gothic style and enlarged in the Decorated style. After much reckless damage in the Civil War and sad neglect in the eighteenth century, it was fully restored in the Victorian era. The three spires, a unique feature among British cathedrals, are familiarly known as the 'Ladies of the Vale' and they provide an imposing focus from all directions, including from the peaceful secluded close, which is one of the most complete in England.

The great display of sculpture on the highly decorated west front screen (1) is mostly Victorian. The beautiful vista of the nave (1285) (2) and vaulted ceiling leads the eye eastwards to the three tall traceried pointed windows of the unusually high Lady Chapel (7), 370 feet to the east.

Opposite bottom: Among the many statues in Lichfield's west front is this statue of St Mary the Virgin and the boy Jesus. The beautiful scrolled door hinges of wrought iron date from 1293.

The three spires of Lichfield Cathedral are known as the 'Ladies of the Vale'. Much restoration work was needed on the west front and spires in the nineteenth century.

At the entrance to the choir (3) George Gilbert Scott placed a magnificent decorated screen by Skidmore during his restoration work after 1856. Dr Samuel Johnson, who lived in Lichfield, and David Garrick, the actor, are commemorated in the south transept (4). Up stairs off the south choir aisle, above the consistory court, is the thirteenth-century Chapel

The nave and choir at Lichfield Cathedral are of roughly the same length. The latter, seen here, was in the Early English style, but was later embellished so that it looks very ornate. This splendid vista culminates in the tall windows of the Lady Chapel. The Shrine of St Chad once stood just beyond the High Altar.

of St Chad's Head (5), from which the gold-covered skull of the saint was exhibited to the people. At the end of this aisle is the poignant memorial (1817) by Sir Francis Chantrey to two little girls killed in a tragic accident at home (6). William de Morgan tiles surround the tomb of Bishop Selwyn, first Bishop of New Zealand, in the fine Lady Chapel (7), whose

Francis Chantrey's monument to 'The Sleeping Children', Ellen-Jane and Marianne, who died in 1812 after a tragic accident. Trying to reach above a fireplace with some flowers, the younger girl's dress caught fire; her sister died, too, trying to save her.

An elongated octagon, the chapter house at Lichfield, built in 1249, is rib-vaulted from a single central pillar. It is approached through a vestibule.

splendid sixteenth-century stained glass windows came from Belgium in 1802. The spot where the shrine of St Chad once stood is marked on the floor just west of here (8). The choir stalls are of the 1850s, as are the splendid floor tiles by Minton with roundels showing events in the life of St Chad (9). Off the north choir aisle is the lovely arcaded vestibule (10), lined with stone seats, through which the chapter house (11) is approached. A central pillar of clustered columns supports the wonderful vault. Among the foliage carved around the bishop's seat can be found a cat which has caught a mouse! The vaulted cathedral library above houses many treasures, including its medieval tiled floor.

The eighth-century St Chad's Gospels are priceless. There are 'Mirror of the Age' Library Tours for which booking is essential. The East End Appeal included the priceless Herkenrode Glass Project, restoring the Lady Chapel and its exceptionally tall windows.

LINCOLN

CATHEDRAL CHURCH OF THE BLESSED VIRGIN MARY

Diocese: most of Lincolnshire. Founded as a cathedral about 1072 (Dorchester 886, Leicester 680, Lindine 678). The USA Foundation promotes Lincoln's ties with North Americans and their historical links.

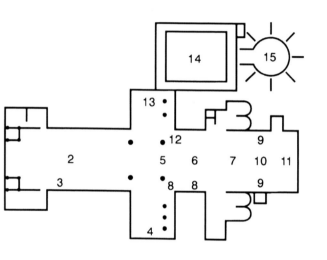

1. West front with the cathedral centre facing
2. Nave
3. Norman font
4. Bishop's Eye rose window
5. Pulpitum
6. St Hugh's Choir
7. Sanctuary
8. Doorway to south choir aisle
9. Ambulatory
10. Angel Choir
11. East window
12. Doorway to north choir aisle
13. Dean's Eye
14. Cloister
15. Chapter house

THE MINSTER CHURCH of Lincoln, founded about 953, was served by mission priests who evangelised in the area. After the seat of the bishop was transferred from rural Dorchester-on-Thames to bustling Lincoln in 1072, its new bishop, Remigius, built a Norman church. Only the incomparable façade of the west front (1), still with superb Romanesque bas-relief, of rare carvings, survived an earthquake in 1185, but the building begun by Bishop Hugh of Avalon is in every respect a masterpiece of English Gothic, a majestic poem in stone, gracing the hill from which much of its stone was quarried. It was completed after his death

The memorable soaring towers of Lincoln Cathedral. The central tower of c.1250 once had a wooden spire (removed in 1548), as had the west towers until 1807.

A ceiling boss is an ornamental carving concealing the join in the rib-vaulting. There are many amid the stone vaulting inside Lincoln Cathedral but this boss is one of several in the wooden roof of the cloister.

by other great men, including Bishop Robert Grosseteste. 150 years later the church was complete, with three huge towers (all once with spires, the central one of 1311 rising to a phenomenal 524 feet). Vast and honey-coloured, it is a wonderful sight from every angle, near and far across the surrounding fertile fenland.

Time is needed to appreciate fully the exuberance and masterful craftsmanship at every turn, with much rich ornament throughout in glass, wood and stone. There is a profusion of dark Purbeck marble, in shafts around the piers in the nave (2) and throughout the arcade above. Note also the Norman font of Tournai marble (3). The fine, traceried rose window, filled with fragments of ancient glass, at the south end of the Great Transept (4) is known as the Bishop's Eye.

The rose window it faces in the north transept is known as the Dean's Eye (13), whose tracery and glass date from the beginning of the thirteenth century (a tour of the restoration workshops is available). Beyond the

In the south transept of Lincoln Cathedral the rose window, known as the 'Bishop's Eye' dates from 1325–50 and replaced an earlier one. It is one of the largest examples of curvilinear tracery. The many leaf shapes bring to mind the biblical text 'The leaves of the Tree are for the healing of the Nations' Its twin, the Dean's Eye, in the north transept, is a fine example of an earlier style called plate tracery.

splendid fourteenth-century pulpitum (5) is St Hugh's Choir (6), built in the last years of the twelfth century, with fine choir stalls, misericords and a 'crazy' asymmetrical vault (see page 268) in which for the first time additional ribs (tiercerons) were added just for the effect. Carved Roman guards sleep at the foot of the arches of the Easter sepulchre in the sanctuary (7). Magnificent stone doorways (8, 12) lead into the choir aisles and ambulatory (9), lined with graceful and unique 'rhythmic' double arcading. Optical illusion, light and proportion arising from an interest in geometry occupied the minds of thinkers like Bishop Grosseteste, the inspiration behind this Gothic architecture. (St Hugh's cathedral had ended in a superb chevet with an ambulatory and radiating chapels in the French fashion.)

The impressive High Gothic nave at Lincoln was completed in the mid-thirteenth century.

The lovely Easter sepulchre of c.1300 at Lincoln is the only one in an English cathedral. The figures are of sleeping soldiers guarding the tomb.

The Angel Choir (10), so called after the carved angels in the spandrels of the tribune arcade, was a worthy setting for the shrine of St Hugh and the tremendous east window (11), the largest and earliest eight-light window in England. On a pillar near the new memorial to St Hugh can be seen the grotesque called the 'Lincoln Imp'. On the north side of the cathedral lies the wooden-vaulted cloister (14), with delightful bosses and a classic colonnade built by Sir Christopher Wren in 1674. The superb ten-sided chapter house (15) is the earliest of the polygonal type. Above Wren's colonnade is the library he rebuilt to house the great collection here, where a copy of Magna Carta used to be kept; it is now in the castle.

A chapter house was for the meetings of the chapter, the cathedral's governing body, which began with a reading of a 'chapter' from the rule book. Lincoln's was the first of the great polygonal chapter houses, a graceful structure built from 1220 to 1235. The parliament of King Edward I met here in 1301.

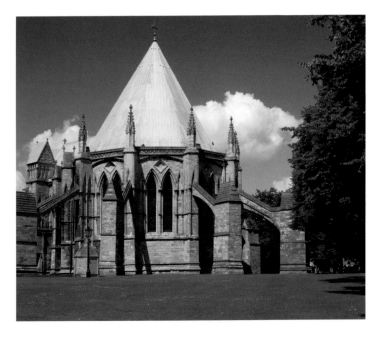

LIVERPOOL
CATHEDRAL CHURCH OF CHRIST

Diocese: most of Merseyside; parts of Lancashire, Greater Manchester and Cheshire. Diocese formed 1880, foundation stone laid 1904. Consecrated 1924. With that centenary in mind the '20 for 2024' campaign is designed to ensure conservation and future mission and ministry of the cathedral.

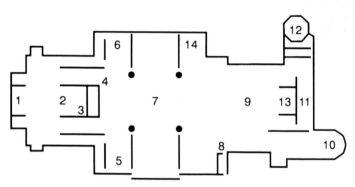

1. 'Benedicite' west window
2. Nave
3. Queen's Stone
4. Lovers' knot
5. Baldachino over font
6. Vast central space
7. Memorial to Giles Gilbert Scott
8. Memorial to the sixteenth Earl of Derby
9. Choir
10. Lady Chapel
11. Ambulatory
12. Chapter house
13. Sanctuary
14. War Memorial Chapel

THIS, THE LARGEST cathedral in Britain, and among the five largest in the world, was finally completed in 1978. A great service of thanksgiving in the presence of Her Majesty the Queen marked this culmination of building over a period of seventy years or so. Guildford and Liverpool are the only two Anglican cathedrals built on new sites in Britain since the Middle Ages. It is built prominently, parallel to the river Mersey, of local sandstone, and the overall impression is one of vastness, the interior permeated by a sense of awe-inspiring

The awe-inspiring grandeur of the fortress-like central tower of Liverpool's Anglican Cathedral dominates Merseyside. At 331 feet it is one of the tallest of church towers. The nave and choir on either side are of equal length. Hope Street links this and the Roman Catholic Cathedral.

space and grandeur, the masterly achievement of the architect. Giles Gilbert Scott was only twenty-two when he submitted his design for what John Betjeman called 'one of the great buildings of the world'. He died in 1960, eighteen years before it was completed.

The view along the nave (2), through the largest Gothic arches ever built, and the central space to the great east window is breathtaking. Set in the right-hand wall of the nave bridge staircase is the Queen's Stone (3), commemorating the completion of the cathedral in 1978. On the opposite side, on the other side of the bridge, is a lovers' knot (4) recording the earlier visit in 1949 of the then Princess Elizabeth and Prince Philip. This is a good place to turn and look at the superb great west window by Carl Edwards (1). At the far end of this transept is the 40 foot high, ornately carved wooden baldachino (5) housing the honey-coloured marble font covered by a tall font cover. Standing within the vast central space beneath the tower, one may appreciate something of the awesome immensity of the building (6). In the middle of the central space (7) is the memorial roundel to the architect, set directly under the soaring tower arches 107 feet high. Further on, to the right in the transept, is the memorial (8) to the sixteenth Earl of Derby – behind one of the tassels of the cushion hides the church mouse! Filling the arches on each side of the choir (9) are the pipes of the largest cathedral organ in use in the world. There is splendid carving in the stone angels and in the wooden stalls: at the feet of each is a carved liver bird. Three tall windows surround the sumptuous reredos in the Lady Chapel (10); before it is a

The so called 'umbrella' vault inside Liverpool Cathedral's Central Tower spreads high above our heads at the staggering height of 175 feet. Twilight Tower Tours for sunset views over city and river are very popular.

The last major work of Dame Elizabeth Frink – 'The Risen Christ' (often known as 'The Welcoming Christ'). A few days before her death in 1993, the sculptor watched on television as her work was installed above the 'west' entrance of Liverpool Cathedral.

Here in Liverpool Anglican Cathedral one is over-awed when gazing upon 'several vast spaces' all at once – nave, west transepts, central tower, east transepts, choir and sanctuary, in local red sandstone.

fifteenth-century Italian figure of a kneeling Madonna by Giovanni della Robbia. The ambulatory (11) leads to the chapter house (12) and then to the sanctuary (13). The great reredos is part of the wall and above it soars the great east window. The colours of several regiments hang above the War Memorial Chapel (14), which contains among other memorials the illuminated roll of honour of Liverpool people who died in the First World War. Just before the death of the sculptor Elizabeth Frink, her figure of the 'Risen Christ' was placed above the 'west' entrance. The victims of the Hillsborough football tragedy are commemorated in the Queen's Walk. Community spirit, ecumenical endeavour and co-operation are legendary in this city. In partnership with the Royal British Legion, the Heroes Path commemorates VE DAY and Second World War veterans.

LLANDAFF

CATHEDRAL CHURCH OF ST PETER AND ST PAUL

Diocese: from the western half of Cardiff to the west of Neath; up to the Head of the Valleys road in the north. Probably the smallest in area and the most populous. Original foundation: mid sixth century.

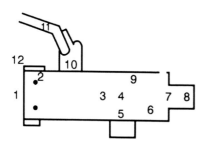

1. West front
2. St Illtyd's Chapel
3. Pulpitum and 'Majestas' figure
4. Gothic arch
5. Celtic cross
6. Presbytery
7. Norman arch
8. Lady Chapel
9. St Dyfrig's Chapel
10. Chapel of St David
11. Processional way
12. Jasper Tower

IN WALES AN early Christian settlement was called a *llan*, still the Welsh word for church or parish. Teilo, a sixth-century monk, ministered here near the river Taff and his *llan* was sited where the cathedral stands today, just north-west of Cardiff. Away from the town, the setting still feels rural among trees, with a green, preaching cross and ruins nearby.

The Norman church was begun in 1120, the notable west front (1) a hundred years later. The church was altered and extended until the Reformation, when the treasures were plundered and dispersed and there followed nearly three hundred years of neglect. In the eighteenth century the attempt by John Wood of Bath to transform the cathedral into what was termed an 'Italian temple' fortunately failed through lack of funds, although what he did build lasted for a hundred years. Llandaff owes much to the nineteenth-century restoration of John Prichard, even though a landmine in 1941

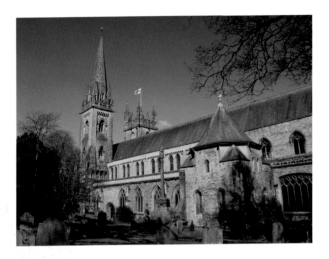

The nineteenth-century Prichard Tower, with its spire, and the Jasper Tower behind, flank the west front of Llandaff Cathedral. John Prichard was a local architect, commissioned to build the tower by Henry VII's uncle, Jasper Tudor, Duke of Bedford. New technology of miniature helicopter drones has been used, as elsewhere, to inspect the exterior of the cathedral.

caused almost complete destruction; among British cathedrals, apart from Coventry, Llandaff endured the most extensive war damage, but here the core of the original church has become part of the new structure.

The most eyecatching feature inside is the pulpitum, a parabolic concrete arch surmounted by 'Majestas', Epstein's figure of Christ in Glory set upon a concrete cylinder, surrounded by sixty-four small Pre-Raphaelite figures (3). The whole design doubles as an organ case, all very original and cleverly conceived to separate the nave from the choir as is normal in a cathedral, but still allowing an uninterrupted view eastwards to the lofty nineteenth-century Gothic arch (4) and the lovely decorated Norman arch (7) which frames the high altar. St Illtyd's Chapel (2) contains the Rossetti triptych 'The Seed of David'. In the south-west corner stands the modern font by Alan Durst with local saints depicted on it. In the south choir aisle near the door to the chapter house is the ancient Celtic cross (5) which is the only relic of the pre-Norman church. St Teilo's thirteenth-century effigy lies in a handsome niche in the presbytery (6). Above the Norman arch (7) and altar is John Piper's window 'Supper at Emmaus'. Beyond the altar is the lovely Lady Chapel (8), beautifully lit through stained glass by Geoffrey Webb, with a medieval reredos enriched with modern bronze panels depicting wild flowers named in Welsh. Burne-Jones designed the porcelain panels depicting the 'Six Days of Creation' in St Dyfrig's Chapel (9). A fine example of the modern renovation and additional new building is the

David Chapel (10), endowed as their memorial chapel by the Welch Regiment, linking the cathedral and the Processional Way (11). Outside, the sovereigns' heads which adorn the south and north walls of the nave should not be missed and the fifteenth-century Jasper Tower (north-west, without a spire) (12) is particularly noble.

Llandaff is a very good example of a cathedral church with a very full parish life, the parishioners being involved in a wide spectrum of activities.

Epstein's figure 'Majestas' and the organ case above a concrete parabolic arch form a pulpitum or screen in Llandaff Cathedral.

LONDON
CATHEDRAL CHURCH OF ST PAUL

Diocese: City of London, most of Greater London north of the Thames; a small part of Surrey. Founded as a cathedral in 604.

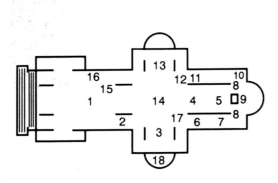

1. Nave
2. 'The Light of the World' painting
3. South transept
4. Chancel
5. High altar and baldachino
6. Statue of John Donne
7. Lady Chapel
8. Sanctuary screens by Jean Tijou
9. American Memorial Chapel
10. Chapel of Modern Martyrs
11. Samuel Johnson's statue
12. Figure of Sir Joshua Reynolds
13. North transept and font
14. Dome
15. Duke of Wellington's monument
16. General Gordon's monument
17. Entrance to crypt
18. Stone inscribed 'Resurgam'

Opposite top: Building the new St Paul's Cathedral took from 1675 to 1710. The architect, Sir Christopher Wren, was 79 when he saw his masterpiece consecrated in 1711.

THIS IS A familiar national shrine. The fifth church on this site was built nearly three hundred years ago when Christopher Wren replaced one of the largest medieval cathedrals in Europe with a classical domed building which has remained unmistakable on the London skyline and appeared especially defiant in pictures of the London Blitz of December 1940.

The Great Fire of 1666 destroyed Old St Paul's and gave Wren his opportunity to rebuild the great cathedral completely in the classical Baroque style. King Charles II supported Wren's ambitious design and the first stone was laid in 1675. Wren was one of the new breed of young architects and his idea of a dome to span the central space partly had its origin in the medieval Octagon and lantern at Ely, where his uncle was Bishop. Here there is an inner painted ceiling, a middle supporting brick cone and an outer lead dome.

The chancel (4) was completed first, then by 1681 the transepts (3,13), by 1684 the nave (1), and by 1686 the west front. The dome (14), the second largest in the world, was consecrated in 1710 and the whole building in 1711, when Wren was seventy-nine.

Previous page: After the Great Fire of London, it was demanded that the ruinous, burnt out Old St Paul's be replaced with a 'large central space beneath an imposing dome' (see page 46) – Wren's inspiration. The chancel was completed first, then the transepts (1681) the nave (1684), and, two years later, the west front.

As with all great churches, the diversity and excellence of the craftsmanship is astounding. As well as enjoying the magnificence of the building, it is worth seeking out Holman Hunt's painting 'The Light of the World' (2) in the south aisle and, just beyond, John Flaxman's memorial to Nelson in the south transept (3). Here the magnificent wood-carving by Grinling Gibbons is first seen in the doorcase, originally part of the choir screen. The superb oak and limewood choir stalls in the chancel (4), the bishop's throne and the organ case (on each side of the choir) are more of his work. The brilliant mosaics above were added at the end of the nineteenth century by W. B. Richmond. The organ was built by the great 'Father' Schmidt in 1695. Modern craftsmen made the splendid baldachino and high altar (5) in 1958. It is dedicated by the people of Britain to members of the Commonwealth forces who died in the two world wars. The statue in the south choir aisle of the poet John Donne (1573–1631) (6), Dean of the cathedral, is remarkable not only because it is the only one to survive the Great Fire, but also because Donne posed in his shroud for the sculptor, Nicholas Stone. The oak altar table in the Lady Chapel (7), formed only in 1959, is Wren's original high altar table and the surround was part of his organ screen. The great craftsman Jean Tijou made the wrought-iron altar screens (8) and the gates at the entrances to the choir aisles. Both the American Memorial Chapel in the apse (9) and the Chapel of Modern Martyrs (10) beyond are poignant reminders of sacrifice. Samuel Johnson's huge statue (11) stands at the entrance to the north choir aisle and on the corner of the north transept is Flaxman's figure of Sir Joshua

Reynolds (12). The north transept (13) displays the colours of the Middlesex Regiment, whose chapel it is: to the west is the font (1727) in blue-veined Italian marble. High in the dome (14) is the intriguing Whispering Gallery. The fresco

paintings on the inner dome done by Sir James Thornhill in 1716–19 depict the life of St Paul. In the centre of the floor under the dome are the Latin words *Si monumentum requiris, circumspice* ('If you seek [Wren's] monument look around'). Monuments to great soldiers including the Duke of Wellington (15) and General Gordon (16) are in the north aisle. The tombs of Wellington, Nelson, Wren and other eminent people and memorials to others, together with the OBE Chapel and Wren's 'Great Model' of the cathedral, are in the crypt (17), which is the largest in Europe. James Horrobin's gate-cum-screen, unveiled on 30th November 2004, commemorates Sir Winston Churchill.

On the pediment above the south door (18) is the word *Resurgam* ('I shall rise again'), an inscription Wren found on a stone in the ruins of the Old St Paul's. In the early twenty-first century this great national shrine has undergone a £40 million restoration to mark its three-hundredth anniversary. The cathedral has a prestigious visual arts programme involving many celebrated artists. In 2010 *Flare II*, a sculpture by Antony Gormley, was installed in the Geometric Stair of the south west tower. St Paul's has also been challenged by controversial issues. During the global financial crisis, when core beliefs of justice and truth were in the media spotlight, the 'Occupy Movement' set up tents in front of this and some other cathedrals.

'Remembering with Hope' – the large congregation of representatives from all walks of life at St Paul's Cathedral for the tenth Anniversary of the 9/11 catastrophe in New York and its aftermath worldwide.

Opposite: The tomb of Admiral Lord Nelson in the crypt of St Paul's Cathedral. The sarcophagus of black marble was made for Cardinal Wolsey, who fell from Henry VIII's favour three hundred years before. This crypt is now an ideal, unique venue for special functions.

MANCHESTER

CATHEDRAL AND COLLEGIATE CHURCH OF ST MARY, ST DENYS AND ST GEORGE

Diocese: most of Greater Manchester, parts of Lancashire. Became a cathedral in 1847.

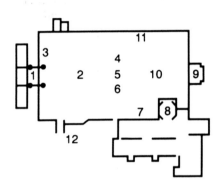

1. West Tower
2. Nave
3. Statue of Humphrey Chetham
4. Angel Stone
5. Medieval choir screen
6. Carving
7. Jesus Chapel
8. Chapter House
9. Lady Chapel
10. Chancel
11. Manchester Regiment Chapel
12. Carving of the Good Shepherd

For a city of Manchester's size and importance, this cathedral does not appear very prominent. It dates from the early fifteenth century, in the Perpendicular style, and it was a collegiate and parish church built on the site of a Saxon church. The cathedral is surprisingly wide because it is now double-aisled: the medieval practice of building chantry chapels on to the aisles had almost doubled its size and when in the nineteenth century space was needed for bigger congregations the chantry partitions were removed from the nave aisles, doubling their width. The cathedral sustained some severe war damage in 1940 and much restoration was needed, including an entirely new Lady Chapel (9) and a fully restored Manchester Regiment Chapel (11), which now has a fine roof in keeping with the nave and choir.

The upper storeys of the west tower were rebuilt in 1867 and its roof was beautifully fan-vaulted (1). The fifteenth-century

Manchester Cathedral. The lofty Perpendicular windows of the clerestory were added after 1485. The west tower was rebuilt in 1867.

nave (2) has unusually wide clerestory windows above the lofty elegant pillars and also an especially fine camber beam roof adorned with bosses and supported at the wallposts by angels holding musical instruments. Against the west wall is the statue of Humphrey Chetham (1580–1653) (3), who founded a school for boys which is now the famous school of music. On the north side of the chancel arch, in front of the unique medieval choir screen (5), is the Angel Stone (4), an eighth-century fragment of a Saxon church. Notice the fine detail in

The beautiful medieval carved screen or *pulpitum* in Manchester Cathedral. Of rare craftsmanship, it was the gift of James Stanley in the 1480s. His family were connected with this church in Tudor times. He was Warden here 1485–1509 and later Bishop of Ely.

Manchester Cathedral has a double-aisled six-bay nave, with wide clerestory windows and a beautifully carved camber beam roof. The choir beyond the screen has extremely fine stalls, their wood carving almost unequalled, also the gift of James Stanley.

the carving of the very beautiful pulpitum (6). The chantries round the choir remain. The Jesus Chapel (7), founded in 1516 and with a lovely sixteenth-century screen, is one of them. Modern murals illustrating the Beatitudes from the Sermon on the Mount have been put into the stone tracery above the double doorway of the chapter house (8). The oldest screen in the cathedral stands at the entrance to the Lady Chapel (9). In the chancel (10) there is much exquisite craftsmanship in wood, including the parclose screens on either side of the high altar, the superb and rare pulpitum (choir screen) dividing the choir from the nave and, most notably, the choir stalls, profusely adorned with carving. Damage caused by Second World War and terrorist bombs has now been restored.

Outside one should note the tall 130 foot west tower (1) and, over the door of the nineteenth-century south porch, the carving of the Good Shepherd by Alan Durst (12). To the north, a short distance away, are the Chetham's Hospital School buildings. To the south-west the old Hanging Bridge is a feature of the restaurant. There have been pilot programmes for the cathedral to host its own television channel. Strong links are being forged with the Muslim community, with inclusion and diversity in mind in the cathedral's overall ministry.

NEWCASTLE UPON TYNE

CATHEDRAL CHURCH OF ST NICHOLAS

Diocese: Northumberland, and parts of County Durham and Cumbria. Became a cathedral in 1882.

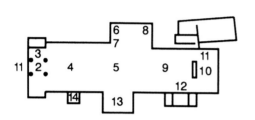

1. Tower crown and lantern
2. Font and canopy
3. Memorial to Admiral Collingwood
4. Nave
5. Pulpit
6. Crypt chapel
7. Organ case
8. St George's Chapel
9. Choir
10. Thornton brass
11. Danish memorial
12. Window commemorating chemist
13. Effigy of unknown knight
14. Medieval stained glass roundel

NEWCASTLE CATHEDRAL is today a focus for much ecumenical ministry at the heart of commercial and industrial Tyneside and the mother church of a large rural border county. The Normans built a church, consecrated in 1091, here at what has been a strategic point by the river since Roman times. It was almost entirely rebuilt in the Early English style in the late thirteenth and early fourteenth centuries; there followed much beautification through the years, culminating in the eyecatching, 'crowning' glory of the 203 foot high tower (1), with its unusual lantern and pinnacles. The clock was added in 1761. John Knox, the fervent Scottish reformer, preached regularly here in 1550–3. A memorial marks the strong ties between Tyneside and Denmark in the Second World War (11) and there is also a modern window above it based on a design by Queen Margrethe of Denmark.

Straight ahead as one enters is one of the cathedral's great treasures, the early-fifteenth-century marble font with its elaborately carved cover in a characteristic local style (2). Near the door is a memorial to the Newcastle-born Admiral Collingwood, Nelson's second in command at Trafalgar (3). The stonework of the nave (4) is unadorned and handsome and the side aisles surprisingly are very wide. When the church became a cathedral in 1882 it was splendidly refurnished in fifteenth-century style. A fine example is the pulpit of Uttoxeter stone (5). Down a few steps in the north transept is the crypt chapel (6), built originally as the charnel chapel to house bones from the churchyard. The splendid organ case (7) was built in 1676 by the great Renatus Harris. The Cunard

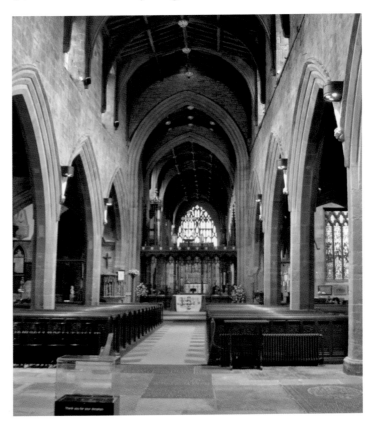

The view of the nave of Newcastle Cathedral to the choir and high altar. A striking feature is that the floor slopes from west to east, almost 18 inches (45 cm). The side aisles are also unusually wide.

The fifteenth-century tower and lovely crown of Newcastle Cathedral. A very distinctive and beautiful Tyneside landmark, the lantern gives inspiration to the cathedral's mission statement: **L**ight of Christ, **A**live, **N**urturing, **T**eaching, **E**cumerism, **R**econciling, **N**ow and in God's future.

The sculpture *Eucharist* by Stephen Cox in Newcastle Cathedral depicts the Holy Trinity expressed in the Broken Bread – a wafer (in alabaster), and the Wine – (an ellipse made of imperial porphyry).

liner *Mauretania* appears in a window in St George's Chapel (8); here also is the colourful Hall memorial. Turning into the choir (9), note Bishop Lloyd's beautiful canopied tomb and the fine nineteenth-century furnishings. In the south aisle turn left to the far end; on the wall is the Roger Thornton brass of 1441 (10), the 'Dick Whittington' of Newcastle. Above it the unusual sculpture by Stephen Cox expresses the Holy Trinity in the broken bread of the Eucharist; the ellipse below is wine in a tilted chalice. Returning west, a window before the south transept depicts a chemist in his shop (12). The oldest memorial in the church is the effigy of an unknown knight in St Mary Magdalene's Chapel (13) in the south transept; the elaborate Maddison memorial here portrays three generations of the family, including sixteen children. In St Margaret's Chapel off the south aisle is a roundel of beautiful medieval stained glass depicting the Virgin and Child (14). Ongoing refurbishment aims to ensure flexibility and further the cathedral's extensive ministry, its worship and witness. *Discovery, Development and Challenge.* are the keynotes of this project entitled 'Common Ground in Sacred Space'.

Opposite: The elaborate tomb chest and canopy of Bishop Lloyd's tomb at Newcastle.

NEWPORT
CATHEDRAL CHURCH OF ST WOOLOS

Diocese: extends from Monmouth to Chepstow; the M4 corridor to Newport, the outskirts of Cardiff, the rural areas of Raglan, Abergavenny and the Herefordshire border. Called the Diocese of Monmouth, created in 1921. Became a cathedral officially in 1949.

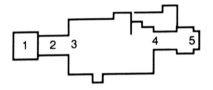

1. Fifteenth-century west tower
2. Lady Chapel (St Mary's)
3. Nave
4. Sanctuary
5. Rose window and mural

The Norman nave arcades of Newport, conveying simplicity and strength.

ACCORDING TO LEGEND, Gwynllyw or Woolos was converted to the Christian faith in the sixth century. Here on Stow Hill, in obedience to a vision, he had a little church built to commemorate his change of heart. The present Lady Chapel (2) probably stands on the site of his church.

The west tower (1) is fifteenth-century, partly built by Humphrey, sixth Earl of Stafford, and high enough to

The sturdy fifteenth-century tower of the Cathedral Church of St Woolos, Newport, is built on a ridge that dominates the city.

give views of the Bristol Channel. It has the largest peal in Wales, with thirteen bells. One enters the fine Norman nave through the imposing, deeply carved late Norman doorway, which is the cathedral's finest feature. The nave (3) is also late Norman with zigzag carving on the arches; the side aisles are in the much later Perpendicular Gothic style. The vista beyond the chancel and sanctuary (4) culminates in the impressive extension of 1960 with a splendid rose window and mural by John Piper (5), instead of the traditional east window found in other cathedrals. This is a lovely church with a number of interesting monuments and a happy blend of ancient and modern. The transition from darkness to light is especially effective as one moves eastwards. The former Church House pub nearby, renamed Cathedral House, is a place for hospitality, witness and increasing engagement with the wider community.

NORWICH

CATHEDRAL CHURCH OF THE HOLY AND UNDIVIDED TRINITY

Diocese: most of Norfolk, small part of Suffolk. Built as a cathedral about 1096 (Dunwich, 630; North Elmham, 673; Thetford, 1070).

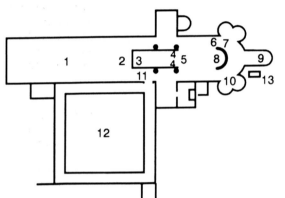

1. Nave
2. Screen
3. Choir stalls
4. Bishop's stall and pulpit
5. Pelican lectern
6. Reliquary arch
7. Norman apse
8. Ancient throne
9. Chapel of the Norfolk Regiment
10. St Luke's Chapel
11. Prior's Door
12. Cloisters
13. Grave of Edith Cavell

THE FIRST CATHEDRAL church of the see of East Anglia lies today beneath the North Sea, off the crumbling Suffolk coast at Dunwich. At North Elmham are a few remains of the

Saxon cathedral which replaced it. However, the present magnificent building was begun by Bishop de Losinga in 1096 after the Normans removed the see to Norwich in 1094. The blending of the Norman Romanesque and Gothic styles is one of the cathedral's most pleasing attributes. Until the Reformation the shrine of the little-known William of Norwich attracted medieval pilgrims. This is also the city of Mother Julian, the fourteenth-century mystic. Imposing against the East Anglian sky, the fifteenth-century spire, second in height only to Salisbury's, rises from the graceful tower – the tallest Romanesque tower in England. The rare exposed flying buttresses of the presbytery confirm the feeling of strength and reassurance at the heart of this historic city, second only to York in the number of its medieval churches.

Opposite bottom: The bosses in the nave at Norwich illustrate themes from the Old and New Testaments. The Romanesque arcades are crowned with a later Gothic vault of 1463.

A stunning blend of styles at Norwich Cathedral. The first spire was burnt in 1272; its replacement blew down in 1362 and the next was struck by lightning in 1463. The present spire dates from the 1480s. The 1362 disaster destroyed the Norman clerestory east end; tall traceried windows were inserted and the necessary but attractive flying buttresses to add support, while the lower level remains Norman – all a very distinctive and beautiful feature.

From the late medieval choir stalls with their extremely fine, often amusing, misericord carvings, we approach England's finest Norman apse with later beautiful clerestory windows above, and more superb vaulted ceilings, for which Norwich Cathedral is famous.

The very long Norman nave (1), even longer than Ely, has a beautiful Romanesque arcade and an equally stunning Perpendicular vault of the fifteenth century with superb bold bright roof bosses. Beyond the screen (2) the medieval choir stalls (to the west of the tower, monastic fashion) with their fine misericords (3) are complemented by the splendid nineteenth-century craftsmanship of the pulpit and Bishop's 'choir' stall (4). The ancient lectern is, unusually, a pelican, not an eagle (5). Over the end of the north choir aisle is the reliquary arch (6), built in 1424 to house relics but now the cathedral treasury. Beyond the high altar is England's finest Norman apse (7), with three chevet chapels, surmounted by an impressive range of huge Gothic windows (the clerestory) and another splendid vault. The unique Ancient Throne, the oldest bishop's throne in England (8), is placed centrally at the top of the steps behind the high altar, as was an early Christian custom. In the chapel of the Norfolk Regiment (St Saviour's Chapel) (9) the beautiful medieval painted panels are of the Norwich school, as are those in the Despenser retable in St Luke's Chapel (10). Look

back at the wonderful carvings around the Prior's Door (11) as you enter the cloisters (12), two-storeyed and among the largest and most notable in the world, then up at the unrivalled, colourful roof bosses. The grave of Nurse Edith Cavell, shot by the Germans at Brussels in 1915, is outside at the far east end (13). There is much more to discover in a stroll around the precincts. Do not miss Pull's Ferry at the watergate to the east, where stone was brought for the building of this extensive Benedictine monastery. The cathedral's development campaign to conserve and improve facilities continues. It was from Norwich that Justin Welby began his *Prayer Pilgrimage* through six dioceses, before his enthronement as archbishop in March 2013 at Canterbury. *The Pilgrims' Trail* here includes the wonderful Herb Garden where workshops are also held. As elsewhere, pastoral care is paramount and the *John Aves Education Project* seeks to assist and empower disadvantaged young people.

Situated on the south side of the nave, Norwich cloisters are among the finest and largest at an English cathedral. The ceiling bosses are extremely fine here also.

Above an arch between the north presbytery aisle and the Norman apse at Norwich, by the site of a former reliquary chapel (now the treasury), there are paintings dating from the early fourteenth century.

The grave of Nurse Edith Cavell, executed by the German authorities in Brussels in the First World War. She had assisted two hundred prisoners of war to escape.

OXFORD
CATHEDRAL CHURCH OF CHRIST

Diocese: one of the largest, over 2200 square miles. Oxfordshire, Berkshire, Buckinghamshire and a small part of Warwickshire. Became a cathedral in 1545 (diocese 1542).

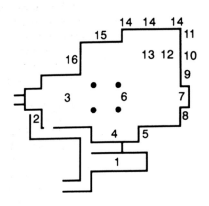

1. Chapter house, shop, treasury
2. Burne-Jones window: 'Faith, Hope and Charity'
3. Nave with unusual double arches
4. Lucy Chapel
5. Becket window
6. Presbytery
7. East end
8–10. Burne-Jones windows
11. Burne-Jones window: Life of St Frideswide
12. Lady Chapel
13. Latin Chapel
14. Fourteenth-century windows
15. St Michael window
16. Jonah window

SELDOM REFERRED TO as Oxford Cathedral, Christ Church, as it is known, is the only chapel of a university college that is also a cathedral church; it is, therefore, also the smallest. St Frideswide ('Bond of Peace'), a Saxon princess, is said to have founded a church here in the eighth century. Her shrine came eventually into the guardianship of Augustinian monks. Until 1525 Christ Church was a monastery called St Frideswide's Priory. Cardinal Wolsey obtained a papal bull to dissolve the priory and had, among other works, demolished four bays of the church to make space for Tom Quad before his fall from favour. In 1546 Henry VIII refounded the college as Christ Church and transferred the Bishop of Oxford here. In the nineteenth century scholars of the Oxford Movement did much to revitalise the Church of England; in the regimental chapel there is a bust of Dr Edward Pusey, one of the leaders.

Entering from Meadow Gate and along the cloisters, turn first through a Norman doorway into the Early English chapter house (1), now both the shop and the diocesan treasury. In the cathedral, just to the left of the south door is the 'Faith, Hope and Charity' window by Burne-Jones, the first of five he designed here (2, 8, 9, 10, 11). The late-twelfth-century nave arches (3) are unusual double ones, with the triforium tucked under each arch; this gives an illusion of height. King Charles I stayed at Christ Church during the Civil War and in the south transept and the Lucy Chapel (4) are several Royalist memorials. The precious medieval window (5) in the chapel here was made in 1320 to commemorate the murder of Thomas Becket.

In the choir and presbytery (6) William Orchard, probably the creator in 1500 of the lierne vault, displayed the virtuosity for which this cathedral is famous, namely the pendants and carved bosses forming stone lanterns, in all a delicate, intricate pattern. The Romanesque style of the east end (7) is part of the nineteenth-century restoration. In the Lady Chapel (12) the remains of St Frideswide's

A unique place of worship – Christ Church is both a university college chapel and Oxford's cathedral. The stone spire, much restored, is early-thirteenth-century, one of the oldest in this 'city of dreaming spires'.

The late-fifteenth-century watching loft or chantry near the shrine of St Frideswide in Oxford Cathedral.

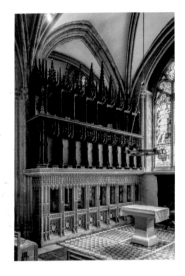

shrine (1289), destroyed at the Reformation, were reassembled in the nineteenth century. Facing it is a large wooden watching loft (to guard the shrine) or a chantry. In the superb east window (11) here Burne-Jones depicts the life of St Frideswide. Three fourteenth-century tombs separate the Lady Chapel from the Latin Chapel (13), which has three fine fourteenth-century windows facing them

Oxford's crowning glory: a stunning array of stone bosses and pendants, foliage and star shapes in the chancel.

(14). Lighting the north transept is the St Michael window by Clayton & Bell (15) and at the west end is the unusual Jonah window (16), which, except for Jonah, is a painting on glass. Apart from its spire, the first built in England, c.1230, this

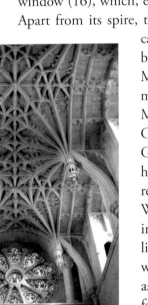

cathedral is hidden among the college buildings and somewhat inconspicuous. Marking the Millennium, an altar made of a block of oak donated by Her Majesty the Queen graces the Peace Chapel. It also commemorates Bishop George Bell, once an undergraduate here, later an outspoken champion of reconciliation in the Second World War. Christ Church has been featured in Harry Potter films and a famous literary connection is through the writer Charles Dodgson, better known as Lewis Carroll of *Alice in Wonderland* fame; from the 1850s onwards he was a student here and then a teacher for most of his life.

PEEL

ISLE OF MAN, CATHEDRAL CHURCH OF ST GERMAN

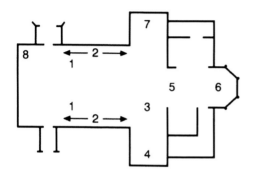

1. Sandstone columns
2. Seven windows commemorating bishops
3. Locally crafted furnishings
4. South transept and King Solomon window
5. Embroidered kneelers
6. Apse and windows portraying Jesus
7. Window portraying Jacob
8. Windows: 'The Crucifixion' and 'The Light of the World'

CELTIC MISSIONARIES, POSSIBLY including St Patrick from Ireland, evangelised here in the fifth century, and from the ninth century until the early sixteenth century the Isle of Man and the Northern and Western (or Southern) Isles were Norwegian dioceses: 'Sodor' in the diocese name Sodor and Man derives from the Norse for Southern Isles. From the thirteenth century the former St German's Cathedral, the mother church of the diocese for five hundred years, was built on St Patrick's Isle at the mouth of the river Neb near the castle. Once the residence of kings, the site was historically the most important in the Isle of Man. A visit there is very worthwhile; the ruins are impressive and memorable. Building continued through the next two centuries. In the late nineteenth century, when the cathedral chapter was established, the Chapel of St Nicholas at

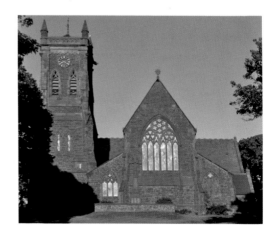

Previous page: The bell tower at the Cathedral Church of St German, Peel, also a parish church. Built in 1879–84, the church was finally consecrated as the cathedral on All Saints' Day, 1st November 1980.

Bishopscourt was designated a procathedral. However, it was not until All Saints Day 1980 that Kirk German, built between 1879 and 1884 to replace St Peter's church, became the new cathedral of the diocese. Uniquely the Bishop is also Dean, as the Cathedral Chapter record shows.

The building is of local stone although the columns are of Cheshire sandstone (1) in the style of those in the old cathedral. Seven windows (2), memorials to bishops, depict scenes in the life of Jesus. Work has gone on to improve the cathedral's ministry, which is extremely varied, both parochially and in the diocese. To this end there has been some sensitive reordering and refurbishment, especially at the front of the nave (3). Many of the new furnishings were made on the island; of special note are the embroidered kneelers (5). A wall hanging commemorates the local millennium (1979). The high altar is backed by an apse (6) with three windows glorifying Jesus, depicting the Transfiguration, the Resurrection and the Ascension and representations of Old Testament characters, the work of J. M. Nicholson RI. The pulpit, font and reredos are of Caen stone. In the north transept a superb window (7) portrays Jacob. In the north-west corner of the nave near the entrance two windows (8), 'The Crucifixion' and 'The Light of the World', command one's contemplation and attention. Nearby, at the west end, is a heritage area with items and artefacts of historic interest.

The original St Germain's Cathedral on St Patrick's Isle, Peel, Isle of Man.

PETERBOROUGH

CATHEDRAL CHURCH OF ST PETER, ST PAUL AND ST ANDREW

Diocese: Northamptonshire, Rutland, part of Cambridgeshire. Became a cathedral in 1541.

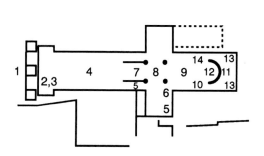

1. West front
2. Elizabethan gravedigger portrait
3. Font
4. Nave
5. South aisle and south transept
6. Chapel of St Oswald
7. Choir
8. Central tower ceiling
9. Presbytery
10. Burial place of Mary, Queen of Scots
11. Norman apse
12. Hedda Stone
13. New Building
14. Tomb of Catherine of Aragon

THE UNCORRUPTED ARM of King Oswald of Northumbria, killed in battle in 642, was one of several sacred relics collected in the eleventh century by the Benedictine monks here at Medeshamstede ('the settlement in the meadows') on the edge of the fertile open fenland. In a battle with the Normans Hereward the Wake caused one of the many fires which ultimately led to the rebuilding of the abbey in its present form in the 120 years following 1118.

The unique west front (1), in essence a portico of magnificent Early English arches, is one of the chief glories here. Much has been written about the classical proportions of the huge arches and gables. The Perpendicular porch of about 1380 inserted in the central arch now houses the cathedral treasury. Inside, just to the left of the original wooden doors

Flanked by buttressing towers with spirelets, at Peterborough the three huge deep arches of the Early English west front create a most dramatic effect. They are not of equal size. The Galilee porch in the centre was added c.1380.

to the cathedral, look for the portrait of the Elizabethan gravedigger (2) and, beyond that, the thirteenth-century marble bowl of the font (3). The long and lofty Romanesque nave (4) lacks a stone vault but has its original painted wooden ceiling of 1220, unique in England, with a striking lozenge design (compare Ely). There is an uninterrupted view eastwards (481 feet) to the apsidal east end (11), the earliest part of the abbey to be built, in 1118; the almost rhythmic flow of the three stages, arcade, triforium and clerestory, is especially impressive here. Next to Durham this is England's finest unspoilt Norman Romanesque interior. Entrances to the foundations of the Saxon church are at the end of the south aisle (5) and in the south transept: here also is the Chapel of St Oswald, with a watching loft to overlook and guard the relic (6). The vaulted ceiling of the central tower (8) beyond the choir (7) is also painted and the coffered wooden vault of the presbytery (9) is highly elaborate. When the central tower had to be rebuilt at the end of the nineteenth century the choir was refurnished with the splendidly carved choir stalls, choir pulpit and bishop's throne, and the elaborate marble mosaic pavement and high altar canopy were installed in the presbytery. Catherine of Aragon, the first wife of Henry VIII, was buried here in 1539 and her tomb (14) is in the north choir aisle. In the south aisle, immediately opposite, is the place (10) where Mary, Queen of Scots, was buried after her execution in 1587 at Fotheringhay, about 10 miles away, but when her son became King James I he had her body moved to Westminster Abbey. Notice the Hedda Stone, from the first Saxon church, behind the altar in the apse (12). This is another rare Norman apsidal east end (11) (compare Norwich), the most complete in England. The cathedral culminates in the so-called New Building (13) of 1496–1508

The Norman tower at Peterborough was taken down in the 1300s and rebuilt, and again in the 1880s. Some of the bosses in the vault may be copies of the original ones.

The so-called New Building (1496–1508) extends eastwards from the splendid Norman apse; it is in Perpendicular style with superb fan-vaulting found in few other places.

in Perpendicular style, the last phase of English Gothic. John Wastell, later the builder of King's College, Cambridge, built this splendid fan-vaulting. On the east wall, commemorative plaques acknowledge the many donors who contributed to the 1996 appeal. Re-cleaning and other emergency work was urgent after the serious fire of 22nd/23rd November 2001, which affected the whole building. A satisfying attribute of Peterborough Cathedral is its vastness and the uncluttered feel about it. The precincts and old buildings are being used imaginatively, with various amenities, linking well with the city centre close by.

PORTSMOUTH

CATHEDRAL CHURCH OF ST THOMAS OF CANTERBURY

Diocese: part of Hampshire, the Isle of Wight. Became a cathedral in 1927.

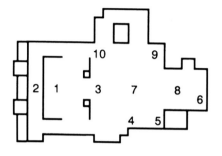

1. Sunken nave with ambulatories
2. West rose window and gallery
3. Tower, Jube gallery, font
4. Navy Aisle
5. Martyrs' Chapel
6. South sanctuary aisle monument
7. Choir
8. Sanctuary and altar
9. Lady Chapel
10. Madonna and Child plaque

EIGHT HUNDRED YEARS ago Augustinian monks built a chapel here dedicated to St Thomas, Archbishop and Martyr, murdered in his cathedral at Canterbury in 1170. In the Middle Ages the low central tower served as a naval

Previous page: The twin west turrets of Portsmouth Cathedral are at the corners of the nave; between them is a rose window and inside, a singing gallery.

The lantern at the top of the cupola on the tower of Portsmouth Cathedral was, for centuries, the first thing seen by home-coming seamen. 'Heaven's light is our guide' is the city motto. This cathedral has been dubbed 'The Cathedral of the Sea'.

watchtower since, even in those days, the town was a significant port linking England with France. After damage in the Civil War King Charles II donated money for restoration; the tower, set at the west end of the old church, again served as a watchtower. A cupola was added later. After the church became a cathedral, work began in the 1930s to enlarge it, to the plans of Sir Charles Nicholson, but was curtailed by the Second World War. Building did not resume until the mid 1980s and was completed by Michael Drury in 1991. Twin turrets now flank the west door and as a whole the building is a pleasing blend of old and new. The cathedral has close links with France, made stronger by recent history.

The splendid nave (1) is square and sunken, with aisles at the same level as the rest of the cathedral. Below the west rose window (2) is a tribune gallery so designed that words and music from here can be heard throughout the cathedral. Beneath stands the Golden Barque weathervane which surmounted the cupola from 1710. Opposite, in the tower (3), is the Jube, a stone gallery from which the liturgy was sung from 1938, and behind it is the splendid early-eighteenth-century organ case. Under the tower is the large and impressive modern font in Purbeck stone. The Navy Aisle (4) was partly paid for by

donations from men of the Royal Navy. A slab of Welsh slate marks the grave of a seaman buried 450 years after he and many others drowned when Henry VIII's *Mary Rose* sank in the Solent in 1545. Ahead is the Martyrs' Chapel (5), where there is a striking statue of St Sebastian and an abstract Death and Resurrection triptych. The upper lancet

The large cruciform font in Portsmouth Cathedral, placed here in 1991, is of ninth-century Greek design.

The new nave at Portsmouth was completed in 1991. The bronze west doors have a 'Tree of Life' motif in the design.

window shows the arms and badges of all countries and units taking part in the D-Day landings in Normandy in 1944. Prominent on the wall of the south sanctuary aisle (6) is the monument to George Villiers, Duke of Buckingham (unpopular favourite of Charles I), murdered in Portsmouth in 1628. The medieval choir (7) was badly damaged in the Civil War by Parliamentary artillery so the furniture, including the magnificent pulpit and the Corporation Pew, date from the rebuilding of the 1690s. A gallery was first added in the early eighteenth century. The exceptionally fine sanctuary (8) at the east end is a notable blend of Norman Transitional and Early English styles. There is now a modern altar

Portsmouth: looking eastwards across the sunken nave towards the tower, gallery and organ; the choir and sanctuary are beyond.

in Purbeck stone by Michael Drury below the ornate tester by Nicholson. On the east wall of the Lady Chapel (9) is a niche containing a thirteenth-century wall painting in which can just be discerned Christ in majesty sitting in judgement. In the north tower transept, on the east wall (10), is another rare and moving treasure, a majolica plaque of the Madonna and Child by the Florentine artist Andrea della Robbia. At the service of thanksgiving for the completion of the cathedral Sir Francis Drake's words were read: '...it is not the beginning but the continuing of a great matter until it be thoroughly finished that yields the true glory.'

Links with continental Europe are strong; Taizé style services are held regularly. This is a cathedral with a lively programme of parish events. Extensive work is underway to provide better facilities, including those for Education and Music. The Cathedral Innovation Centre, the first of many it is hoped, provides opportunities for the launching, developing and expanding of businesses and enterprises.

RIPON

CATHEDRAL CHURCH OF ST PETER AND ST WILFRID

Diocese: Since Easter Day 2014 part of the amalgamated diocese of West Yorkshire and the Dales (with Bradford and Wakefield). Became a cathedral in 1836 (also briefly in Saxon times).

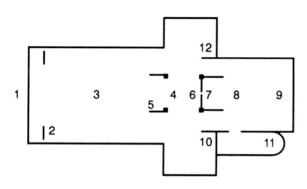

1. West front
2. Font
3. Nave
4. Central tower
5. Crypt
6. Pulpitum
7. Carved wooden hand
8. Choir
9. East window
10. South transept
11. Chapel beneath chapterhouse
12. Markenfield Chapel

For hundreds of years Ripon Minster was one of several such centres in the diocese of York. The first church was built between 671 and 678 by Wilfrid, then Bishop of York, the 'Star of the Saxon Church', who was also associated with Chichester. Wilfrid's arguments for the Roman as opposed to the Celtic tradition of the Christian faith in England at the Synod of Whitby in 664 did much to win the day. He established the minster as one of the foremost and grandest stone buildings in Europe. The part that remains today, his crypt (5), a simple barrel vault 9 feet high at the centre and well-built in dressed stone, is one of the oldest parts of any cathedral; here Wilfrid displayed sacred relics brought back from Rome. It is still a very evocative place. Wilfrid's shrine in the later church attracted many pilgrims. His joyful return to his people is enacted annually with a man playing Wilfrid mounted on a horse. The founders of Fountains Abbey, near Ripon, before setting out on their

Ripon Cathedral from the east; the squat central tower, with the two west towers, had a spire three hundred years ago. The tracery of the east window seen here makes it one of the finest in Britain (compare Carlisle).

enterprise, worshipped here on Christmas Day 1132.

The graceful yet austere west front (1), with its tall lancet windows and twin towers, was added from 1220 to the lovely church that had been begun about 1154 in the Norman Transitional style (when rounded arches began to give way to pointed ones). There was later building in various Gothic styles, culminating in the Perpendicular, seen in the wide dignified nave (3). The mixture of styles is most strikingly seen in the central tower (4), which has two rounded and two pointed arches, and in the north transept and the north arcade of the choir. There is a twelfth-century font (2) in the south-west tower and a Tudor one in the south aisle. The stone pulpitum (6), surmounted by the organ, has an angelic musical band and dates from c.1494 although the figures are modern.

On the chancel side of the screen is a small gallery, the organ seat, from which protrudes a carved wooden hand for beating time for the choristers (7). The choir (8) was beautifully enhanced in 1286 in the Decorated style; the geometrical tracery and size of the great east window (9) make it one of the finest in Britain. Exceptionally fine, too, is the late fifteenth-century craftsmanship in the elaborate carving of the stalls and misericords. The painted bosses in the ceiling are earlier. At the east end of the south choir aisle, the Chapel of the Holy Spirit has a modern screen of aluminium. The staircase in the south transept (10) leads to the library, once the Lady Chapel, where early printed books and manuscripts are kept. Beneath the chapter house is a small simple chapel, once the Norman undercroft (11). In the north transept the Markenfield Chapel is a perfect example of Norman Transitional building (12).

A famous tradition in Ripon is the nightly curfew and the setting of the watch at 9 p.m. each evening, when the Wakeman blows his horn in the market place. Ripon Cathedral has a busy parish life. An 'emerging vision' is at the heart of the strategy 'Growing God's Kingdom' as it seeks to develop its extensive ministry.

Opposite bottom: The Saxon crypt of Bishop Wilfrid's cathedral, dedicated in 672 and one of the oldest parts of any cathedral. Relics and other treasures bought back from a pilgrimage to Rome were placed here to help the faithful focus their prayers. It is still a place for quiet prayer and contemplation today.

The Early English west front of Ripon Cathedral is plain and somewhat austere. The main distinguishing feature of this period is the narrow lancet window. Since 2012 Great Glass Doors grace the entrance, featuring scenes from the life of Bishop Wilfrid, who founded the cathedral here nearly 1350 years ago.

ROCHESTER

CATHEDRAL CHURCH OF CHRIST AND THE BLESSED VIRGIN MARY

Diocese: west Kent and part of Greater London. Founded as a cathedral in 604.

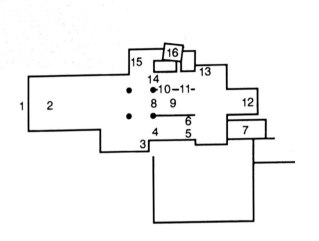

1. West door
2. Nave
3. South transept
4. Stairs to crypt
5. South choir aisle
6. Wooden vestry
7. Chapter room
8. Nave altar and screen
9. Choir
10. Sculptured monk's head
11. Painting of wheel of fortune
12. Presbytery and high altar
13. North choir transept/St William memorial
14. Pilgrim Steps
15. North transept
16. Bishop Gundulph's tower

THE DIOCESE IS the second oldest in Britain. Paulinus, the first Archbishop of York, was buried here in the ancient crypt; so too was St Ithamar, the first Englishman to become a bishop. A bronze line marking the apse of the Saxon church can be seen just inside the west door (1). A new cathedral and a Benedictine monastery were established in 1080 by the Norman bishop Gundulph, whose tower (16) is the earliest work here. William of Perth, murdered by his servant while on his way to the Holy Land, was buried here in 1201 in a tomb that became famous for healing miracles and the focus for pilgrims. Their gifts swelled the funds for further building.

To the side of the splendid and exuberantly carved west doorway and its sculptured tympanum (1), one enters the

small (for Norman Romanesque) yet impressive and spacious nave (2), with huge pillars and splendidly embellished capitals, arcades and triforium. With the money raised by pilgrims' offerings at the tomb of William of Perth, a start was made on rebuilding in the Early English Gothic style. The choir was enlarged, a new choir and the transepts were built. Fortunately the money ran out before more than two bays of the nave could be altered and the Norman arcades were saved. Among the many memorials in the south transept (3) is one to General Gordon of Khartoum. The windows are in honour of Royal Engineers who died in the Peninsula and at Waterloo. At this point the full beauty of the north

The lovely Early English crypt at Rochester. The 'lanes of light' impressed the novelist Charles Dickens. The earlier, Norman part of the crypt is plainer.

The west front of Rochester Cathedral is an outstanding example of late Romanesque architecture. Especially fine is the carving of the old doorway. The Saxon cathedral was situated near the present west end.

Previous page, top: Rochester Cathedral is overlooked by the Norman castle (right). The Norman cathedral incorporated both a monastery and a parish church. Nearly five hundred years earlier, in 604, a bishopric and Christian community were established here on the banks of the River Medway in the kingdom of Kent.

transept (15) can be seen. In the south choir aisle are the stairs down to the crypt, one of the largest, an ancient and evocative place (4). Except for a small Norman section, it is, uncommonly, Early English; the several aisles forming 'lanes of light' impressed Charles Dickens when he was writing his last novel *Edwin Drood*. Up the other steps from the south choir aisle (5), leading first to the medieval wooden vestry (6), there is a good view of the superb fourteenth-century doorway to the chapter room (7); on the wall to the left of it is the memorial to Charles Dickens, closely associated with this city. Beyond the nave altar and screen (8) the thirteenth-century choir (9) is enclosed; unusually the walls are solid and decorated with fleurs-de-lis and 'leopards'. There is some very ancient woodwork and a well-preserved thirteenth-century painting of the wheel of fortune (11). The sculptured monk's head (10) is one of many finely carved heads throughout the church. The dark marble Gothic shafts here and in the presbytery (12) have a sombre beauty. St William is now

represented only by a plain slab in a corner of the north choir transept (13). The Pilgrim Steps (14), worn thin by countless feet, descend into the north transept (15), where in June 2004, one thousand four hundred years after the foundation of the cathedral, a fresco painted by Sergei Fyodorov, 'Water and the Spirit', depicting the baptism of Christ and that of King Ethelbert of Kent by St Augustine, was dedicated. A fresco is a painting done on wet plaster, and this one is said to be the first true example completed in an English cathedral for eight centuries. Erasmus stayed in the old bishop's palace on College Green with Bishop John Fisher, martyred in 1535 and commemorated in the cathedral.

A new project 'Ancient Stones and Untold Stories', made possible by the Heritage Lottery Fund, enables the story of the cathedral to be told creatively and imaginatively. The 'Hidden Treasures Fresh Expressions' project focuses on the famous crypt and library and their possible future development in the interests of the cathedral's ministry.

The Screen at the Crossing, between Nave and Choir in Rochester Cathedral, with figures of founders and benefactors. The Norman builders under Bishop Gundulph started at the east end (1077–1108). There were changes from the 1150s onwards and some ornamentation was added, resulting in a most impressive nave.

ST ALBANS
CATHEDRAL AND ABBEY CHURCH OF ST ALBAN

Diocese: Hertfordshire and Bedfordshire. Became a cathedral in 1877. Site of the beheading of Alban, the first martyr in Britain c.209. Saxon foundation, 793.

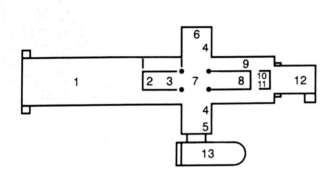

1. Nave
2. Roodscreen
3. Choir
4. Transepts
5. Arches with Roman tiles
6. Stained glass by Alan Younger
7. Norman tower
8. High altar reredos
9. Ramryge Chantry
10. Shrine of St Alban
11. Tomb of Duke of Gloucester
12. Lady Chapel
13. Chapter house

The Shrine of St Alban in St Albans Cathedral. It was on this site that Alban, the first British martyr was beheaded in the third century. Persecution persists worldwide today and modern martyrs are commemorated in this cathedral.

Built on the site of the martyrdom in 209 of the Roman citizen Alban, the monastery became the premier abbey in England. In the twelfth century St Albans Abbey provided the only English Pope, Nicholas Breakspear, Adrian IV. The chronicler Matthew Paris, a monk here in the thirteenth century, produced an illuminating record of events; as St Albans is close to London, the abbey frequently received important guests. From the Reformation

to the nineteenth century the building deteriorated. Even so it became the cathedral of a new diocese in 1877. Lord Grimthorpe's strong-minded and sometimes wilful restoration nevertheless saved from utter ruin the building used as a parish church and a school. The monastery is no more.

The thirteenth- and fourteenth-century wall paintings in Europe's longest medieval nave (1) are among the finest in England; the Benedictine monastery had a high reputation for its school of painters. The mixture of Norman Romanesque and Gothic architecture seen throughout the abbey is immediately apparent in the nave. The roodscreen, which effectively isolates the nave, was built in 1350 (2). The wooden panelled ceiling of the choir (3) is probably fifteenth-century. Of the Saxon abbey there are baluster shafts high up in the transepts (4); a few arches showing reused Roman tiles from nearby Verulamium can be seen high in the south transept (5). In contrast modern stained glass by Alan Younger enhances the large circular Victorian window in the north transept (6).

The west front of St Albans Cathedral was largely redesigned and rebuilt in the 1880s by Lord Grimthorpe, but the Norman tower of 1080 is the oldest cathedral tower in England. The exceptionally long nave is shorter only than that of Winchester.

The murals of the Crucifixion on the west side of the Romanesque pillars in the nave of St Albans Cathedral are among the finest wall paintings of the 1200s. Each pillar had an altar so that the many monks of this foremost of monasteries could say Mass regularly in what was then their abbey church.

The massive tower is the oldest of the great cathedral towers (7): the exterior is faced with distinctive Roman bricks salvaged from the ruined town. The high altar reredos (8) dates from 1484, the statues from the 1890s. Above is the earliest painted wooden vaulted ceiling. On the north side stands the beautiful Ramryge Chantry (9), fan-vaulted in stone; it was the last thing built here before the Reformation. East of this is the shrine of St Alban (10), still a focal point for pilgrims and rehallowed in May 1993; a quaint medieval watching loft of oak overlooks the shrine. The tomb of Humphrey, Duke of Gloucester (died 1447), with a splendid thirteenth-century iron grille, is opposite (11). The Lady Chapel (12) of *c.*1320 was used as a schoolroom for three hundred years until it was restored in the nineteenth century. A new era began with the building of the new chapter house (13) on the site of the old in the early 1980s. The varied ministry and enterprises

of this vibrant parish-church cathedral cover a wide field in an effort to witness, as Alban, the first British martyr, did, to the 'true and living God who created all things'. The project 'Alban, Britain's First Saint – Telling the Whole Story' aims to develop and ensure this cathedral and parish church's ministry in many spheres, such as worship, pilgrimage, hospitality and education. A good example of conservation is the proposed reconstruction of the Shrine of St Amphibalus who, welcomed by Alban, was able to lead him to faith in Jesus Christ.

ST ASAPH
CATHEDRAL CHURCH OF ST ASAPH

Diocese: the north-east corner of Wales, from the Conwy valley in the west to the border of Cheshire in the east; covers the archdeaneries of St Asaph, Wrexham and Montgomery. Probably founded in the early sixth century. Became a cathedral under Canterbury in 1143. As one of the smallest cities, in 2012 it was granted city status as part of the Queen's Jubilee Celebrations.

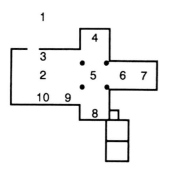

1. Monument to Translators of Welsh Bible
2. Nave
3. Iron chest
4. Chapel of the Translators
5. Central tower
6. Choir
7. Presbytery, high altar and east window
8. Lady Chapel window
9. Effigy of Bishop Anian II
10. Grave slab depicting greyhound and hare

IN THE SIXTH century St Kentigern (St Mungo in Glasgow) placed his disciple Asaph in charge of the monastery here by the river Elwy. He died in 596 (the year before Augustine reached Canterbury) and his body was venerated for many years. In 1282, during the Welsh wars of Edward I and Llewelyn, the Norman church was destroyed. Money was raised for rebuilding by sending 'on tour' a precious gospel manuscript; £95 6s 101/4 d was collected, a vast sum then! This building, probably completed by 1381, was burnt by Owain Glyndwr in 1402. The golden era was at the end of the sixteenth century when, with others, Bishop William Morgan published his translation of the Bible into Welsh in 1588. There is a copy in the cathedral library. All this endeavour, and work on the Book of Common Prayer by others, is commemorated by a fine national monument north of the church (1). During the Puritan Protectorate the cathedral was desecrated and used to house animals; all the records were destroyed. The neglect of many years was at last mended in the nineteenth century by George Gilbert Scott. St Asaph is the smallest medieval cathedral in England and Wales and also one of the oldest. Like St David's, it stands at the heart of both a city and a village. In 1920 the Church in Wales was disestablished and, once separated from the Province of Canterbury, it had its own archbishop and constitution. At the beginning of the twenty-first century an Archbishop of Wales (the eleventh) was chosen as the 104th Archbishop of Canterbury, leader of the Anglican Church worldwide.

St Asaph Cathedral, dominated by the massive thirteenth-century tower. An unusual feature is the two distinctive kinds of stone which unfortunately react together, eating each other away!

Enter through the north-west door into the nave (2), which has simple dignified arches and unadorned pillars: the clerestory windows are of 1403. Immediately ahead is an iron offering chest made by Robert Davies of Croes Voel in 1738 (3). A chapel in the north transept is dedicated to the Translators (4). Beyond the massive central tower (5) are the choir (6), with fine pinnacled fifteenth-century stalls with canopies, and the presbytery (7), much restored in the nineteenth century. Bishop Morgan is buried beneath the bishop's throne. The Victorian reredos of Derbyshire alabaster was given during the restoration of the 1870s and the intriguing painted window replaced an earlier one, parts of which are now in the Lady Chapel window (8). In a niche in the left-hand pillar here is a lovely seventeenth-century Spanish Madonna carved in ivory. There is a small treasury in an alcove in the south wall. In the south aisle, beyond the thirteenth-century effigy of Bishop Anian II (9) is an engraved grave slab depicting a greyhound chasing a hare (10).

The poignant, thought-provoking sculpture *The Naked Christ* is by Michelle Coxon. It is in this diocese that, most appropriately, the Bible Heritage Museum at the once-redundant St Bueno's Church at Llanycil near Bala tells the historic and engaging story of a young girl, Mary Jones; in 1800 she walked miles to buy a bible. Her determination and resolve were the inspiration for the founding of The British and Foreign Bible Society. In the twenty-first century the '2020 Vision' – for growth in discipleship and mission – is behind the project 'Datgloi Ein Potensial – Unlocking Our Potential'.

The pillars of the nave arcade in St Asaph Cathedral lack capitals but they pervade a simple dignity; with the clerestory windows dating from 1403 there is a restful beauty in this holy place, one of the smallest of cathedral churches.

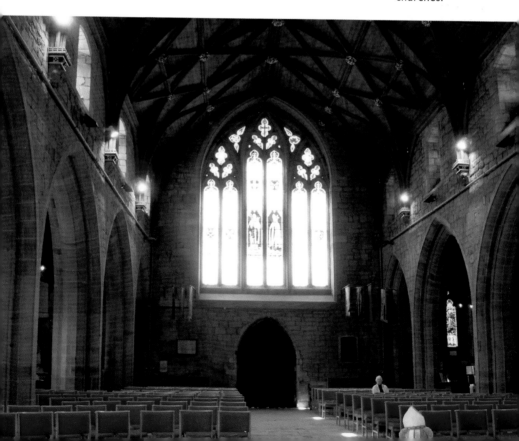

ST DAVID'S
CATHEDRAL CHURCH OF ST DAVID

Diocese: Carmarthenshire, Pembrokeshire, Cardiganshire and a small part of west Glamorgan. Founded as a cathedral church probably in the early sixth century, it is both a parish and a cathedral church. City status was conferred by the Queen in 1995.

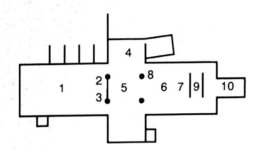

1. Nave
2. Pulpitum
3. Tomb of Bishop Gower
4. North transept
5. Choir
6. Parclose screen
7. Tomb of Edmund Tudor
8. Shrine of St David
9. Holy Trinity Chapel
10. Lady Chapel

Opposite:
The ceiling of the tower of St David's Cathedral is painted with the names and coats of arms of many of the bishops responsible for the building of the cathedral over the centuries. The choir stalls are beneath it.

SINCE THE TIME of St David, patron saint of Wales, in the sixth century the church here, set in a hollow in the lonely valley of Glyn Rhosyn, has suffered damage from warfare, fire and even earth tremor. Nearby are St Non's Well and the holy place, once 'bathed in brilliant light', where the saint was born. All this is evoked again inside this beautiful cathedral amidst rugged coastal scenery.

The nave arches and pillars (1), alternately circular and octagonal, are Norman Romanesque of the late twelfth century. The rare and lovely wooden ceiling is of Irish oak (sixteenth-century) with large pendants. The beautiful early fourteenth-century Decorated pulpitum (2), one of the finest medieval stone screens, also contains the tomb (3) of its builder, Bishop Gower. Above are a twentieth-century organ case and hanging rood or cross. The famous musician Thomas Tomkins (1572–1656), born in St David's, is honoured in the north transept (4) by a memorial in the form of a choir

St David's Cathedral is of the usual cruciform design. The original low tower collapsed in 1220 (not an uncommon occurrence). The third and latest stage of the tower dates from the early sixteenth century. This made the somewhat 'hidden' cathedral more conspicuous from the surrounding hills.

organ case. The central space beneath the beautifully vaulted tower is the choir (5); there is much elaborate wood carving here in the fifteenth-century stalls and the bishop's throne; the Royal Stall for the Sovereign in the choir is unique. A rare parclose screen (6) at this point is a fitting entrance to the presbytery; in the centre is the tomb of Edmund Tudor, grandfather of Henry VIII (7); the thirteenth-century shrine of St David (8) may be seen from the north choir aisle. To the right of the high altar, above which are lancets filled with pictorial mosaics (1871), are some very rare wooden sedilia. The ceilings of both the tower and the presbytery are most impressive. Beyond the high altar in the Holy Trinity Chapel (9), bones once believed to be those of St David, but now thought to be of St Caradog, are kept nearby in a recess. In the wonderful fan-vaulted ceiling are the arms of Henry VII. The beautiful Lady Chapel (10), now much restored, is nearly seven hundred years old. Today's pilgrims find this memorable cathedral and its surroundings restful and rewarding, an

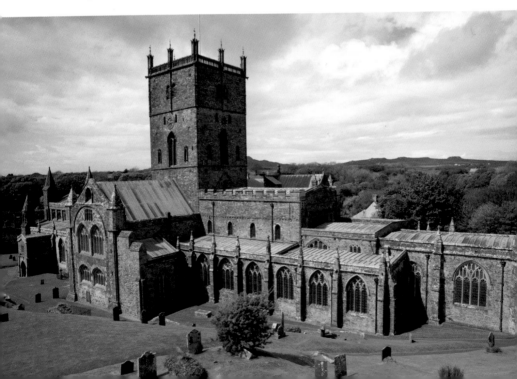

inspiring place, the cradle of the Christian faith in Wales. For this reason special appeals have been launched to improve facilities and aid conservation of this beautiful historic site. These include the Gatehouse, Cloisters and West Front projects. The long-closed Caerbwdi quarry, about a mile away, was reopened in 1996 to provide stone for present and future needs. The restored Shrine of St David was rededicated on St David's Day, 1 March 2012. In the niches are icons of saints with a painted canopy above. Pilgrimages to St David's have been popular for centuries; there is now a special centre in the city to promote education and pilgrimage.

Eastwards from the choir, above the High Altar are three lancets filled with golden mosaics by Salviati; dating from 1871, at the centre is the Crucified Christ, the Christian Church is depicted (left) and Jewish Synagogue (right). Above are four lancet windows; the ceiling is an ancient elaborately painted camber beam roof.

ST EDMUNDSBURY
CATHEDRAL CHURCH OF ST JAMES

Diocese: most of Suffolk and one parish in Essex; called the diocese of St Edmundsbury and Ipswich. Became a cathedral in 1913.

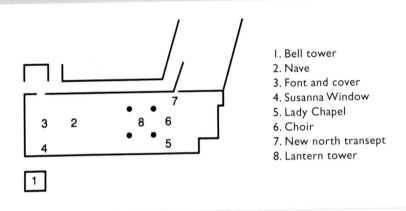

1. Bell tower
2. Nave
3. Font and cover
4. Susanna Window
5. Lady Chapel
6. Choir
7. New north transept
8. Lantern tower

Opposite:
The modern central tower in Gothic style together with the east end of St Edmundsbury Cathedral, seen from the Abbey gardens. At 150 feet and completed in 2005, it has been called 'a spiritual beacon for the new millennium'.

Thirty-four years after the gruesome martyrdom in 869 of the young King Edmund of East Anglia by Viking pirates, his followers brought his headless body to Beodricsworth, known today as Bury St Edmunds, hence 'St Edmundsbury'. In time a magnificent church was built; the huge abbey and monastery, now in ruins, became the greatest in England, covering a vast area and well worth a visit. Formerly the main gateway and one of the finest buildings of its period, the imposing Norman bell tower (1) next to the cathedral stands before the remains of the ancient abbey's west front. It was here on St Edmund's Day 1214 that the barons swore at the high altar of the abbey church to make King John sign Magna Carta.

The cathedral was formerly the parish church of St James, built five hundred years ago in the Perpendicular style by John Wastell, the famous architect who built King's College, Cambridge. It was under his direction that the majestic

Perpendicular nave (2) was built. The present, brightly coloured nave roof was made in the 1860s in characteristic East Anglian hammerbeam style by Sir George Gilbert Scott, who also designed the splendid font (3); the cover was given as a memorial to local men who died in the First World War. The Susanna Window (4) contains some fifteenth-century Flemish glass. Most of the rest of the magnificent glass in the nave was made by Clayton & Bell. In the Lady Chapel (5) there is a lovely little chamber organ made by Henry Holland in 1790. The choir (6), which replaces the third

chancel in the life of this church, together with the tower and transepts, is a twentieth-century addition eastwards by Stephen Dykes Bower to enhance this 'mother of Suffolk churches' and render it large enough for cathedral services. Around the walls of the choir are the coats of arms of the barons appointed to enforce the terms of Magna Carta. The winged buttresses of the splendid bishop's throne are carved to represent the wolf guarding the head of St Edmund. In 1999 work began on the new central tower and north transept (7). The Gothic-style lantern tower (8) – 'A spiritual beacon for the new millennium' (HRH the Prince of Wales) – 150 feet high, the new song school and other facilities here beautify and enhance this cathedral church and its ministry. There are strong local links with the United States, dating from the Second World War.

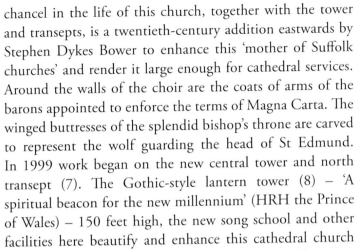

The new east end of St Edmundsbury Cathedral is the inspiration of the late Stephen Dykes Bower, architect here from 1943–88.

As part of the Millennium 2000 Project there was some new building – The Chapel of the Transfiguration (consecrated 2009) the East Cloister (2009) and the Crypt Treasury (2012). The Song School is in the new Cathedral Centre. A reminder of historic origins *The Martyrdom of St Edmund*, a painting by Brian Whelan, is in the Lady Chapel. A stroll through the Abbey Gardens (Green Flag awarded) and the Pilgrim's Herb Garden, is most pleasant and memorable.

SALISBURY

CATHEDRAL CHURCH OF THE BLESSED VIRGIN MARY

Diocese: most of Wiltshire, most of Dorset, part of Hampshire. New cathedral started in 1220. Consecrated 1258 (diocese 1078, Sherborne 705). In 1991 this was the first cathedral to have girl choristers; they were also wholly independent of the boys.

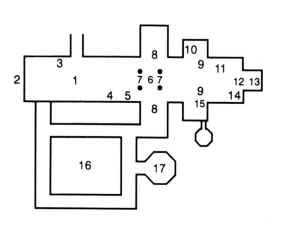

1. Nave
2. West window
3. North aisle
4. South aisle
5. Tomb of William Longespée
6. Tower and spire
7. Buckled piers
8. Girder arches
9. Choir transepts
10. Morning Chapel
11. Audley Chantry
12. Sanctuary
13. Trinity Chapel
14. Hertford tomb
15. Bridport monument
16. Cloisters
17. Chapter house

IN 1220 HERE at New Sarum, the 'new' town, a splendid cathedral church was begun amidst the water meadows, a pleasant place in contrast to the bleak inhospitable conditions 2 miles to the north at Old Sarum, where the Normans had built a castle and a cathedral, the foundations of which may still be visited. This 'new' cathedral, largely completed in thirty-eight years, is entirely Gothic. Apart from the Decorated cloisters (16) and the spire rising superbly to 404 feet and finished about 1315, it is all Early English. St Osmund, a Norman bishop and great administrator who completed the first cathedral on the chalk hill at Old

Salisbury Cathedral's splendid spire, completed c.1315, rises above a superb Decorated tower. It weighs 6400 tons and is 404 feet high – a graceful medieval tour-de-force. This cathedral is the only one (other than St Paul's) the main part of which was completed to the design of one man and without a break. Abseilers have undertaken conservation on the spire. In recent years Peregrine falcons have nested in the tower.

Sarum, was reinterred in the new cathedral and after he was canonised in 1475 his shrine became a place of pilgrimage. Salisbury became a centre for music and liturgical reform. Even after the Reformation the choral tradition continued and the devout poet and country parson from neighbouring Bemerton, George Herbert, loved to attend services. The stunning view of the spire across the water meadows has been immortalised in the paintings of John Constable. The Close is the largest and probably the most beautiful in England.

The design in white Chilmark stone punctuated with shafts of dark Purbeck marble has a purity and a simple austerity which make this perhaps one of the best Early English buildings (1). In the eighteenth century the fine medieval stained glass was unfortunately mostly

Opposite: The nave at Salisbury: dark Purbeck marble shafts contrast with the purity of the white Chilmark stone. The simple but somewhat austere beauty in the arcade and vault show elegance of proportion and design.

Evoking reflection in 'stillness, ever flowing' – William Pye's 2008 cruciform font. The text 'I have called you by name, you are mine' is from Isaiah 43: 1.

removed but that in the west window (2) is splendid; it was recomposed in 1824 from medieval glass. The oldest clock in England, made c.1386 and in use until 1884, stands in the north aisle (3). The tombs neatly lined up along the south aisle stand on the ledge just above floor level. The vistas from this aisle (4) are wonderful; the play of light is often unforgettable. Note the tomb of William Longespée (5), King John's half-brother and the first person to be buried in the cathedral. The Decorated vaulting of the tower (6) was added when the tower and spire were built in the mid fourteenth century. The great weight (6400 tons) to be supported caused the piers to bend, as can be seen (7), and in c.1450 the north and south transept arches were reinforced with girder arches (8). Even earlier the great burden was seen to be forcing out the main walls, so strainer arches were built in the entrances to the choir transepts (9). The fine windows of the Morning Chapel (10) are mainly by Powell of Whitefriars and the wooden doors of the aumbry are thought to be Saxon. Fine fan-vaulting covers the lovely Audley Chantry in the north aisle (11); at the end of the aisle is the George Herbert Window. Standing near the sanctuary (12), it is rewarding to view the whole building. East of the sanctuary is the oldest and most unusual part of the cathedral, the beautiful Trinity Chapel (13), with delicate columns and very pointed

arches. The rich colours of the window commemorate twentieth-century prisoners of conscience. Between the chapel and the Hertford tomb (14) is a marble slab marking the tomb of St Osmund and his former shrine. Just before the south choir transept (15) is the splendid carved monument

Made about 1386, and said to be the oldest in England, the clock operated by these works was once in the central tower of Salisbury Cathedral.

In the Trinity Chapel at the east end of Salisbury Cathedral the vibrant colours of the windows commemorate Prisoners of Conscience of modern times. A candle usually burns here for all suffering persecution.

to Giles de Bridport, who died in 1262. He was bishop here when the cathedral was consecrated in 1258. Outside to the south lie the cloisters (16), the largest in England and perhaps the finest, which lead to the chapter house (17). The central pier divides into sixteen branches to support a splendid fan-vault. The finest of four surviving copies of Magna Carta may be seen in the chapter house. Ken Follet's bestselling book *The Pillars of the Earth* was partly inspired by this cathedral. The glass roof (an inspired design) of the shop and refectory off the cloisters, allows an unforgettable view of the spire.

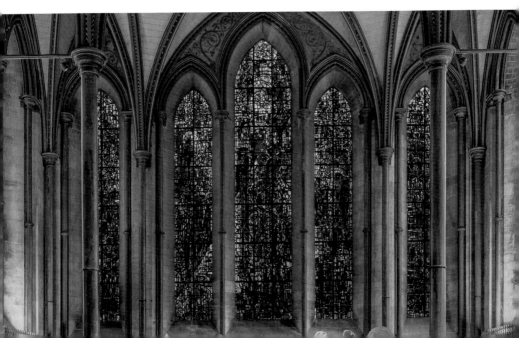

SHEFFIELD

CATHEDRAL CHURCH OF ST PETER AND ST PAUL

Diocese: most of South Yorkshire, parts of the East Riding, West Riding and north Lincolnshire. Became a cathedral in 1914. An active, stimulating parish church cathedral. In 2007 a Community Resource was opened while the 'Gateway Project' (2013/14) gave impetus to the cathedral's wide-ranging ministry.

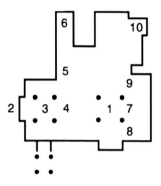

1. Crocketed spire
2. Great window
3. Lantern tower
4. Nave
5. St George's Chapel
6. Chapel of the Holy Spirit
7. Chancel
8. Shrewsbury Chapel
9. St Katherine's Chapel
10. Chapter house

THIS IS A church of ancient origin, founded as a parish church in the twelfth century in the 'open space' by the river Sheaf. The chancel and the sanctuary date from the rebuilding of the fifteenth century (Perpendicular style) as does the fine crocketed spire (1). The lantern tower (3) was added in 1966 when extensions to the cathedral planned before the Second World War were finally completed.

The graceful entrance, narthex and west end date from 1966: the great window (2) is composed from the former west window and other glass from the earlier building. The lantern, glazed in rich colours, suggests the Crown of Thorns. The nave (4) was rebuilt in the early nineteenth century and extended later. On the left, St George's Chapel (5) is devoted to the memory of servicemen and contains the colours of HMS *Sheffield*, the Coldstream Guards and the Hallamshire

At the west end of Sheffield Cathedral's nave is the impressive 1960s Lantern in the tower; the star shape at its centre brings to mind the Crucified Christ's 'Crown of Thorns'. The abstract glazing is the work of artists Amber Hiscott and David Pearl.

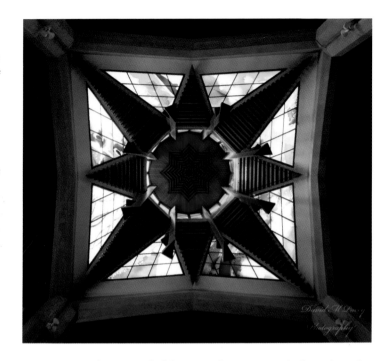

Regiment. The remarkable Sword Screen is believed to be unique. Through the arches behind the altar can be seen the lovely Te Deum window of the Chapel of the Holy Spirit (6) beyond. Ahead and towards the tower is the fifteenth-century part of the church: the chancel (7), with its splendid medieval roof with carved and gilded bosses and angels, and the chapels on either side. The east window is a memorial to a local poet and educationalist, James Montgomery. His many hymns include 'Hail to the Lord's Annointed'. To the south is the Shrewsbury Chapel, the Lady Chapel (8). The tombs of two Earls of Shrewsbury are here: the alabaster effigies of the fourth Earl and his wives (c.1538) are particularly fine. On the south wall here is a thirteenth-century scratch dial or mass clock of the old parish church. To the north is St Katherine's Chapel (9), dedicated to the ministry of women in the church. The top of the unusual altar is pre-Reformation and has been restored after use as paving. The story of Sheffield, the city of steel, and the cathedral is told in stained glass windows in the chapter house (10). Designed by Christopher Webb, it is a story which today involves this cathedral in a special ministry to vulnerable people. The latter is further realized in the Cathedral Breakfast and Archer Project and Resource Centre, all part of the development project which includes providing facilities of all kinds for the disadvantaged and homeless. John Wesley, founder of the Methodist Society, preached to such people in the eighteenth century in Paradise Square. He is portrayed in a window here. There is also much to discover in the purpose-built Crypt Chapel. Through the 'Aurora Training Scheme' young people and lay ministry are developed by the YMCA and Church of England in partnership with Cliff College and the Methodist Church.

At Sheffield cathedral the modern architecture to the left may be of a very different style, but it complements the older building surprisingly well.

SOUTHWARK

CATHEDRAL AND COLLEGIATE CHURCH OF ST SAVIOUR AND ST MARY OVERIE

Diocese: Greater London south of the Thames, part of Surrey. The nave was the parish church from 1614. Became a cathedral in 1905. A strong sense of ministry to marginalised people. In the 1960s Non Stipendiary Ministry was first pioneered in this diocese.

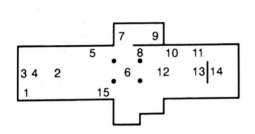

1. *Marchioness* memorial
2. Nave
3. West window
4. Marble font
5. Monument to John Gower
6. Crossing
7. North transept
8. Stilted arch into aisle
9. Harvard Chapel
10. Monument to John Trehearne
11. Wooden effigy of a knight
12. Choir
13. Bishop Fox's screen and tomb of Lancelot Andrewes
14. Retro-choir
15. Shakespeare's monument and window

THE SAXON CHURCH on this strategic riverside site was probably quite large. In 1106 a new church was founded and called St Mary Overie ('over the river' – from the City) and served by Augustinian monks as a daughter community in the diocese of Winchester. Today it stands in a somewhat restricted setting amidst warehouses and commercial buildings, an oasis of calm on the busy South Bank.

To the left as one enters, in front of thirteenth-century arcading is a memorial to the victims of the sinking of the *Marchioness* in the Thames in 1989 (1). The impressive nave (2) was rebuilt in the medieval Gothic style at the end of the nineteenth century; at its core this is London's oldest Gothic building. The west window by Henry Holiday (3) and other windows by Kempe were installed at this time, as was the black marble font by Bodley (4); the roof bosses on the west wall are medieval. Among several interesting monuments around the church is that of the poet John Gower in the north aisle

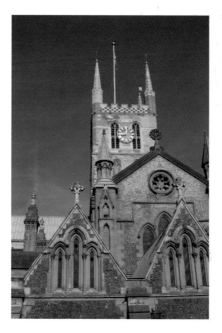

Southwark Cathedral and its precincts, though on a restricted site, are an oasis of calm. In the Millennium Courtyard on the north side, by the river, are amenities opened by Dr Nelson Mandela on 28th April 2001. They include a multi-media exhibition, called 'A Long View of London', alluding to the drawing made by Wenceslaus Hollar at the bend of the River Thames in 1638.

(5). Hanging in the centre of the crossing is a huge brass candelabrum of 1680 (6). Much of the north transept (7) is original thirteenth-century with fragments of Norman work. There is a curious stilted arch (8) into the north choir aisle and to the left is the Harvard Chapel (9), commemorating John Harvard, after whom the American university is named and who was born in Southwark in 1607. Here stands the splendid Gothic tabernacle by Pugin. Further along is another splendid monument, to John Trehearne (10), and next is one of the oldest wooden effigies in England, of a knight (11). Both the choir (12) and the retro-choir were built after a fire at the beginning of the thirteenth century. The choir is a fine example of Early English style furnished largely in the nineteenth and twentieth centuries. Note Bishop Fox's superb stone screen of 1520 (13) and to the right the tomb of the famous scholar Lancelot Andrewes. The Early English retro-choir (14) is wonderfully proportioned and of a high order, the finest architecture of the period in London. Sir Ninian Comper designed the furnishings. Shakespeare's

The Great Stone Screen (1520) behind the High Altar in Southwark Cathedral; it separates the sanctuary from the retrochoir further east. The figures date from 1905. The retro choir boasts some of the finest Early English Gothic in London.

monument (1912) and window (1954) (15) are in the south aisle, beyond the transept; the famous dramatist knew this area well and his Globe Theatre (now re-created by Sam Wanamaker, who is also commemorated here) stood in the locality.

The Queen's Diamond Jubilee in 2012 is marked here by a commemorative stained glass window and the *Choirbook for the Queen* – the best of choral music by British composers – was launched here. The cathedral maintains an important ministry in this busy commercial area of the capital, not least in the sphere of education for young and old.

The monument to William Shakespeare in Southwark Cathedral. Near to the Globe Theatre, it was once his parish church. Behind the figure is a relief of the Southwark townscape.

SOUTHWELL

CATHEDRAL AND COLLEGIATE CHURCH OF THE BLESSED VIRGIN MARY

Diocese: Nottinghamshire, a tiny part of South Yorkshire, but known as the Diocese of Southwell and Nottingham. Became a cathedral in 1884. Often known as the 'Village Cathedral' and 'a best-kept secret'. Called Southwell (Su-thall) Minster rather than Cathedral.

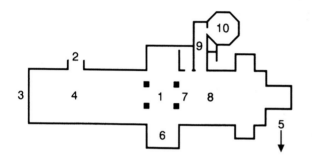

1. Central tower and crossing
2. North porch
3. West front
4. Nave
5. Ruins of old palace
6. Roman paving
7. Choir screen
8. Choir
9. Passage to chapter house
10. Chapter house

THERE IS PAVING of Roman origin (6) in the south transept and evidence of the Saxon church which stood here in the seventh century may be seen in the north transept. A hundred years before the Norman Conquest the manor was granted to the Archbishop of York and remains of the palace (5) remind us of this close link. A college of priests was founded here and the Saxon church became 'York's Minster at Southwell'. This building was begun *c*.1108. From the outside

The unusual segmented arch with bold Norman Romanesque chevron carving above the south transept door at Southwell Minster.

The Romanesque western towers, nave, central tower and north transept of Southwell Minster are almost unchanged since the twelfth century, but the great west window was inserted in the fifteenth century. One characteristic 'porthole' window can be seen in the north transept.

Southwell Minster is an excellent example of a Norman minster comprising, west of the chancel, a stocky central tower (1), porthole-like windows at clerestory level in the transepts and nave, a rare Norman north porch with fine decoration (2), zigzag patterning on the transept gables and, except for a later medieval window, a typical west front (3), still with two spired towers. The Norman pyramid steeples would have been of wood. Inside one appreciates the beauty of the west or Angel window.

In the nave (4) the fine Norman arcades draw the eye to the huge Romanesque arches with cable mouldings at the crossing (1). The imposing figure of *Christus Rex* hangs in act of blessing. The graceful Decorated, three-arched choir screen (7), with its intriguing collection of caricature-like sculptured heads, prepares one for the elegant Early English Gothic choir (8), built in the 1230s to replace the Norman choir, which was rather small. In the screen are six canopied stalls with fine

Some of the splendid Decorated carved capitals, 'The Leaves of Southwell' at the entrance to the magnificent chapter house at Southwell Minster.

misericords; the choir stalls are nineteenth-century. Below the splendid eighteenth-century candelabrum is the lectern, which in the sixteenth century was hidden for safety in the lake at Newstead Abbey. Usually in the south choir aisle are the Stations of the Cross by Jonathan Clarke. However, the paramount glory here is the octagonal chapter house (10), with its sumptuous stone carvings familiarly known as the 'Leaves of Southwell'. The passage from the north choir aisle, the vestibule approach (9) and the doorways are also part of an exuberant display of mythical portraits, of animals and birds as well as humans, amidst a profusion of foliage – oak, vine, hawthorn, hop, ivy, and others. The new Education Garden has a number of special areas, such as woodland developed to link with the famous stone carvings, 'The Leaves of Southwell', in the Minster. This and the Sensory Gardens are near the old Archbishop's Palace, an added attraction here.

TRURO

CATHEDRAL CHURCH OF ST MARY

Diocese: Cornwall, the Isles of Scilly and one parish in Devon; founded in 1877 (cathedral started 1880). Despite its medieval appearance both inside and out, this cathedral is a masterpiece built from the 1880s onwards.

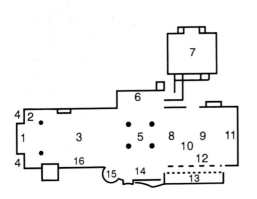

1. Narthex
2. Chapel of Unity and Peace
3. Nave
4. West towers
5. Central tower
6. North transept
7. Chapter house
8. Choir
9. Sanctuary
10. Bishop's throne
11. Retro-choir
12. South choir aisle
13. St Mary's Aisle
14. South transept
15. Baptistery
16. Window depicting John Wesley

IN THE SO-CALLED Dark Ages after the Romans had left Britain in the early fifth century, Celtic saints upheld the Christian faith here in the west when much of Britain returned to paganism. In 994 a cathedral was founded for Cornwall at St Germans but both this diocese and that of Crediton in Devon were later united under Exeter. Truro's splendid cathedral, which is the masterpiece of the architect J. L. Pearson, is built mainly in the Early English Gothic style of the late twelfth and early thirteenth centuries, and executed by fine Victorian craftsmen. It stands on the site of the parish church of St Mary, first built in the 1250s, whose south aisle was fully incorporated into the new cathedral and still functions as a parish church within it.

One enters at the west end, where the narthex of 1991 (1) leads to the Chapel of Unity and Peace (2). The nave (3) was dedicated in 1903. The west towers (4) were completed in 1910. At the point where the nave and the chancel meet there is a slight inclination of the cathedral to the left, necessary to allow the links with the south aisle of St Mary's. In the north transept (6) is John Miller's painting 'Cornubia – Land of the Saints', marking the centenary in 1980. The chapter house of 1967 (7) may be reached from this transept. From beneath the central tower and spire (5), rising to 250 feet and Cornwall's memorial to Queen Victoria, there is a superb view of the choir (8) and sanctuary beyond (9). The famous Father Willis organ here is admired for its power and wonderful sound. The paving is of lapis lazuli and Italian marble. The Bath-stone reredos behind the high altar is the work of Nathaniel Hitch. The bishop's throne (10) is an ornate masterpiece of carving in teak and the choir stalls, also teak, are each surmounted by a statuette of a saint in limed oak. The retro-choir (11) forms an ambulatory linking the choir aisles. Nearby in St Margaret's Chapel is a modern 'Calvary' by the celebrated Craigie Aitchison. Parallel to the south choir aisle (12) is the ingenious narrower aisle

All aglow above its city. 'A little bit of France in Cornwall'. Truro Cathedral with its three fine towers and spires rises majestically above the city's rooftops. It is built appropriately of Cornish granite with dressings of Bath stone; unfortunately the latter erodes easily.

The reredos at Truro rising above the High Altar is of Bath stone with scenes on the theme of sacrifice; at the centre the ultimate sacrifice of the Crucified, Risen and Ascended Jesus is depicted.

linking the cathedral with the medieval St Mary's Aisle (13), which serves as the parish church. The south transept (14) is itself a memorial to Bishop Benson, the first Bishop of Truro and later Archbishop of Canterbury. He devised the famous Service of Nine Lessons and Carols, for Christmas Eve, first used in the humble makeshift 'cathedral' here in 1880. The stained glass in the fine rose window, and much of the other glass, is by Clayton & Bell. The impressive vaulted baptistery (15) is a superb example of Victorian Gothic architecture. The window in the south aisle depicting John Wesley (16) is a fitting commemoration in this diocese where, in the 1880s, Bishop Benson prayed for Christian unity with the mainly Methodist miners at Gwennap Pit. The Breton 'Pieta', the Crucified Lord in His Mother Mary's arms, is the oldest work of art in the cathedral. This is very much a cathedral in the style of those in northern France, where the architect, J. L. Pearson, was inspired by what he saw. As there, so here, this cathedral church is a focal point at the heart of the city, surrounded by the busy world. The 'Inspire Cornwall Project' promotes the county's heritage in Music, Art, Education and the Natural World, while the 'Cross of St Pyran Award' is given to unsung heroes who have served Church and Community faithfully over many years.

WAKEFIELD
CATHEDRAL CHURCH OF ALL SAINTS

Diocese: Since Easter Day 2014 now part of the Diocese of West Yorkshire and the Dales (with Bradford and Ripon/Leeds). Became a cathedral in 1888. Today, as part of one of the most heavily populated dioceses, it is a 'living cathedral that inspires and radiates hope'.

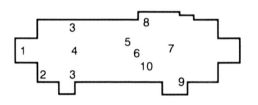

1. Tower and doorway
2. Font
3. Windows by Kempe
4. Nave
5. Pulpit
6. Chancel screen
7. Choir
8. Organ case
9. Saxon preaching cross
10. Cross-legged Madonna

THIS CHURCH HAS passed through various stages of building since its origins in Saxon times, through the Norman period and the Middle Ages. The exterior is very much of the Perpendicular period and there is a superb fifteenth-century tower with a lofty spire (1) 247 feet tall, the highest in Yorkshire. From the 1850s George Gilbert Scott restored the church, removing the old galleries and pews and rebuilding the spire. After the church became a cathedral J. L. Pearson planned the extension to the east end, which was dedicated to Bishop William How, a much loved priest of the nineteenth century, the first bishop of the diocese and the writer of many popular hymns. The Memorial Hall near the cathedral

is in memory of a highly respected bishop of more recent times, Eric Treacy, well-known for his love of railways.

Perhaps the most remarkable feature of this cathedral is the series of stained glass windows. Beginning with those in the south nave wall (3), twenty-four out of twenty-nine are by C. E. Kempe, the first installed in 1872 and the last in 1911, four years after his death. The Early English doorway (1) dates from Scott's restoration – it should have been Perpendicular! The initials CR II on the font (2) indicate that it was installed at the Restoration; the elaborate cover came later from another church. The nave pillars are an interesting

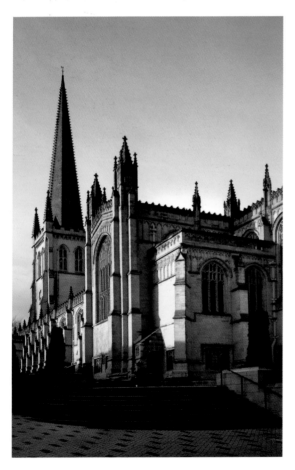

mixture (4) and there is a different number on each side; some have clearly been increased in height, some are Norman and others stand on Norman bases. The fifteenth-century roof is flat and its bosses have intriguing carvings. Look for the Yorkist symbol of a falcon in a fetterlock. Work from the fifteenth century onwards is beautifully combined in the chancel screen (6), culminating in the Crucifixion scene by Sir Ninian Comper, added in 1955. There is interesting woodwork in the choir (7), including some fifteenth-century misericords. The magnificent organ case in the north choir aisle is of 1720 (8). All around, and

There have been various phases of refurbishment at Wakefield Cathedral ensuring flexibility for worship and imaginative use of this sacred space. The chancel screen is of several periods and above it the cross (or rood) by Ninian Comper is of the mid 1950s.

beyond the splendid reredos, the roof is fine stone lierne vaulting of the twentieth century. Look also for the replica of the Saxon preaching cross (9), which probably stood near the first church, and the poignant young cross-legged Madonna and Child by Ian Judd (1986) (10), in what was originally Our Lady's Quire, now the Lady Chapel. It was once also a private chapel of the Pilkingtons, as the elaborate marble memorial recalls. This cathedral plays a vital role in the community and diocese. Its mission statement, based on 'SPIRE', is witness to the good news of the Gospel – 'Serve, Praise, Inspire, Reflect, Educate' – and this is true of all cathedrals. 'Rediscovering our Heritage – Renewing the Cathedral' is a strategy foremost in the life of this cathedral as it engages the wider community in city and diocese with the good news of God's love. In a new initiative the 'Pop Up Cathedral' travels round the new diocese reaching people who otherwise would not be aware of the Church's mission.

Opposite: Wakefield Cathedral has the highest spire in Yorkshire (247 feet). With the tower, it was completed in 1420 and recased in the 1860s by George Gilbert Scott.

WELLS

CATHEDRAL CHURCH OF ST ANDREW

Diocese (called Bath and Wells): Somerset, a tiny part of Dorset. Seat of the first bishop here in 909; Bishop of Bath and Wells from the mid thirteenth century onwards.

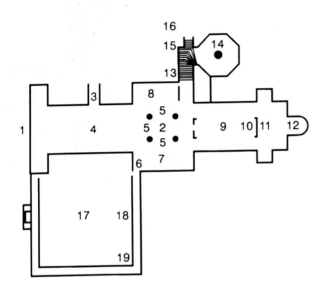

1. West front
2. Central tower
3. North porch
4. Nave
5. Scissor arches
6. Carved capitals
7. Saxon font
8. Astronomical clock
9. Presbytery
10. Golden Window
11. Retro-choir
12. Lady Chapel
13. Stairway to chapter house
14. Chapter house
15. Chain Bridge
16. Vicars' Hall and Close
17. Cloister
18. Ancient library
19. Doorway to moat

THIS CATHEDRAL IN a small city, with the lovely Mendip Hills close at hand and the ancient pilgrimage centre of Glastonbury not far away, has a peaceful setting. In the Middle Ages the vicars choral who deputised for canons (this was never a monastery) had their own community life; many of the buildings associated with them still remain intact and in use. The saintly seventeenth-century bishop Thomas Ken was one of the 'Seven Bishops' acquitted in 1688 of sedition against James II and eventually released to popular acclaim. He is also well-known as a hymn writer.

The west front (1), a masterpiece of English Gothic

architecture, is an inspiring façade, an array of mostly medieval statues, while the majestic central tower (2) has been likened to a pinnacled crown, befitting this queen among cathedrals. Work began *c*.1180, and it took about eighty years to finish most of this, the first truly English Gothic cathedral. Beyond the lovely north porch (3), the nave (4) is especially beautiful when the sun's rays enhance the cream colour of the locally quarried Doulting stone. The unique and ingenious scissor arches (5) were inserted in 1338–48 to prevent the fall of the central tower after it had been heightened after 1313 (a hint of the saltire cross of St Andrew perhaps). The capitals in the nave and transepts are lively with carved stiff-leaf foliage and amusing scenes: on one pier a man with toothache, in the south transept (near the door leading to the cloisters) the story of a man and a boy stealing fruit, and many more (6). The Saxon font (7) from the earlier cathedral stands in the south transept. The fascinating late fourteenth-century mechanical and astronomical clock in the north transept (8) still works.

The west front of Wells Cathedral is the finest in Britain, with its row upon row of statues. The façade is very wide and sculptures extend over the whole of it – a magnificent 'Te Deum in stone'. There are nearly 400 of them: apostles, prophets, martyrs, saints, and Christ in Majesty in the centre at the top (see also page 31).

In reflective mood. From the palace moat the cathedral seems to glisten in the tranquil water; the stone of the cathedral has a special beauty in this early morning light.

The remarkable and lovely stairway to the chapter house at Wells Cathedral, built c.1255. The stairway carries on upwards to the Chain Bridge and the Vicars' Hall, and the Vicars' Close beyond, a very ancient street.

The choir and stone-traceried walls of the presbytery (9) are wonderfully lit by the faithfully restored Golden Window (10) of fine old glass, c.1340, and the misericords of about the same time are among the finest. At the far eastern end, beyond the bright and almost ethereal retro-choir (11) with its delicate slender pillars and interlacing vaulting, is the Lady Chapel (12) with a wonderful star vault and beautiful medieval glass in the upper parts of the windows. Beyond the north transept is an unusual 'heavenly stair' approach (13) to the exquisite vaulted chapter house (14), finished in 1319; it has a crypt-like undercroft. Leading off the stairway is the Chain Bridge (15), with the Chain Gate beneath. It was built over the road in the fifteenth century to connect the cathedral with the Vicars' Hall and Close (16), reputedly the oldest complete inhabited street. Even though there were never monks here, there is a cloister (17), rebuilt in the fifteenth century when the library (18) was added. The thirteenth-century doorway (19) in the south-east corner leads to the moated bishop's palace.

'Theology in Wells' is a stimulating programme of study which attracts people of various ages and degrees of interest.

Necessity as the mother of invention is seen in this ingenious answer to an architectural problem. The roof and the western great scissor arch, one of three constructed in 1338–48 to support the tower at Wells Cathedral.

WINCHESTER

CATHEDRAL CHURCH OF THE HOLY TRINITY, ST PETER, ST PAUL AND ST SWITHUN

Diocese: most of Hampshire, a tiny part of Dorset, the Channel Islands. Cathedral founded in the mid seventh century (cathedral originally at Dorchester in Oxfordshire, diocese 676).

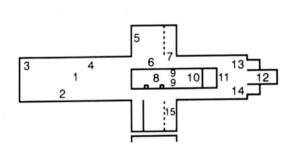

1. Nave
2. Chantry chapel of William of Wykeham
3. Jane Austen's grave
4. Font
5. Chapel of the Epiphany
6. Chapel of the Holy Sepulchre
7. Norman crypt entrance
8. Choir
9. Saxon mortuary chests
10. Reredos
11. Retro-choir
12. Lady Chapel
13. Medieval floor tiles
14. Bishop Langton's Chantry
15. Silkstede Chapel

ROMAN CHRISTIANS MAY have worshipped on this site; the king of the West Saxons founded a minster here – the excavated outline of the Saxon church may be seen today – which became a cathedral in c.670. Winchester became the capital of England. King Alfred the Great was buried here. He was taught by Swithun, the famous bishop and saint (died 862). A cloudburst while Swithun's bones were being moved in July 971 gave rise to the familiar notions about a wet English summer! In the Middle Ages Winchester and neighbouring St Cross Hospital were on the route of many pilgrims; the so-called Pilgrims' Way runs from here to Canterbury. The Norman cathedral was begun in 1079 and

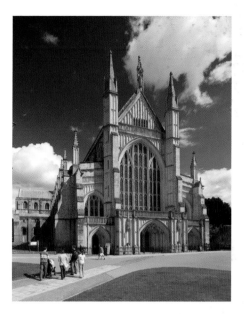

The remodelling of the west front of Winchester Cathedral was completed in 1410. The great west window was already in place about 1360. The somewhat subdued exterior belies the glories of the interior – the English Perpendicular Gothic style at its best.

the powerful grandeur of the early Romanesque building can still be seen in the transepts. The superb nave (1) is the brilliant achievement of Bishop William of Wykeham's architect, William Wynford, who remodelled the arcades from 1394 by means of refacing the Norman work with Perpendicular; the soaring pillars and arches actually encase the earlier walls. The splendid vault completed the work. The bishop is commemorated in the finest (2) of the chantry chapels – for which the cathedral is famous. The grave of the novelist Jane Austen is in the north aisle (3) and just beyond it is the black marble font (4) carved with miracles of St Nicholas. The Chapel of the Epiphany (5) and the remarkable wall paintings dating from about 1180 in the Chapel of the Holy Sepulchre (6) give some idea of how the Norman cathedral looked. In winter the Norman crypt (7) has flood water, reminding us that the Norman builders were indeed daring to construct on a marsh! In the early twentieth century the diver William Walker worked alone in the dark to strengthen the foundations. His small bronze statue is outside Bishop Langton's Chantry (14).

Opposite: Architecture, the handwork of creative artists and music all combine in celebration and worship. Soaring Perpendicular Gothic arches and pillars encase much of the original Norman masonry of the nave at Winchester (see also pages 42–5).

Winchester is noted for its chantry chapels, such as that of Cardinal Beaufort (1404–47), in a worthy position near St Swithun's shrine.

Anthony Gormley's impressive statue 'Sound II' is in the crypt, entered from the north transept. The tomb supposed to be that of King William Rufus, killed by an arrow in 1100, stands in the choir (8). The beautifully carved early-fourteenth-century choir stalls are among the oldest in the land. In the presbytery mortuary chests containing bones of Saxon bishops and kings can be seen on top of the screens at each side (9). The splendid high altar screen or reredos (10) is late-fifteenth-century (compare St Albans). The earliest additions and alterations to the cathedral can be seen beyond the high altar in the lovely Early English retro-choir (11), which housed the shrine of St Swithun (now marked by a modern monument) and still has the largest area of

The Norman arcade and gallery of the north transept at Winchester. Both transepts show us what the Norman cathedral was like. There are three distinctive levels or storeys – the main arcade, the gallery and the clerestory at the top. Compare this with the Gothic nave as it is now (page 222).

medieval floor tiles in England (13). Four of the cathedral's celebrated chantry chapels are here. Just west of the Lady Chapel (12) stands the statue of Joan of Arc. Off the south transept, in the Silkstede Chapel (15) is the gift of the anglers of England and America commemorating Izaak Walton, a window inscribed 'Study to be quiet'. The library and the museum, entered from the south transept, contain treasures such as the twelfth-century Winchester Bible and original statuary from the Great Screen. The tradition of education and art, marks of the Benedictine monastery here, continue; there have been many scholars connected with this great church. Although most of the monastic buildings have disappeared, a walk around the close on the south side is recommended. 'Kings and Scribes, the Birth of a Nation' is an initiative for the conservation of the cathedral and its treasures. People of all ages are at the heart of what the clergy and laity here seek to do to the Glory of God.

In Winchester Cathedral's crypt, which floods frequently owing to the fact that the Normans built it on a marsh, 'Sound II' – a life-sized figure of a man – contemplates water in his cupped hands. In 1986 the sculptor Antony Gormley fashioned this in lead from a plaster cast of his own body.

WORCESTER

CATHEDRAL CHURCH OF CHRIST AND THE BLESSED VIRGIN MARY

Diocese: most of Worcestershire. Founded as a cathedral about 680.

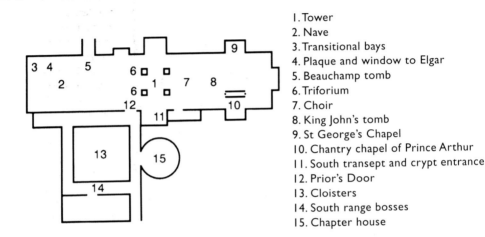

1. Tower
2. Nave
3. Transitional bays
4. Plaque and window to Elgar
5. Beauchamp tomb
6. Triforium
7. Choir
8. King John's tomb
9. St George's Chapel
10. Chantry chapel of Prince Arthur
11. South transept and crypt entrance
12. Prior's Door
13. Cloisters
14. South range bosses
15. Chapter house

IN SAXON TIMES there was a cathedral here and a Benedictine monastery was founded by St Oswald in the tenth century. In 1084 Wulstan, who was the only Saxon to remain a bishop after the Norman Conquest, built a substantial cathedral in the Norman Romanesque style, with a fine crypt, still to be seen. In the Middle Ages pilgrims flocked to the shrines of the saintly bishop and St Oswald. King John requested burial here and his tomb (8), with figures of St Oswald and St Wulstan beside him, stands before the high altar. Extensive rebuilding and restoration took place throughout the Middle Ages. The setting by the river is incomparable.

The handsome tower (1), which is truly central, is the earliest in the Perpendicular style, completed in the 1370s. Most of the nave (2) dates from about 1320 but the two westernmost

Worcester Cathedral has the earliest Perpendicular central tower. Charles II is said to have watched the Battle of Worcester from it. In the foreground are ruins of monastic buildings such as the monks' dormitory. Since the cathedral is by the river, other old buildings nearby include a fourteenth-century water gate and a ferryman's house.

bays on the north side (3) are quite different and Transitional – part Norman and part Early English. Perhaps the plague of the Black Death delayed completion of the work. In this aisle a window and plaque commemorate the great composer Sir Edward Elgar (4), who was born near Worcester. Almost opposite the north door is the colourful Beauchamp tomb (5). Another strange building feature can be seen in the triforium at the end of the nave (6), where there are stone ribs to buttress the tower so that it would not collapse again as it had done in

The stained glass in the cloister windows at Worcester provide a unique pageant of church history.

1176. The east end, with the choir, lofty retro-choir and Lady Chapel beyond, is one of the best examples of the Early English style; the triforium arcading is particularly lovely, with many original carvings in the spandrels, a black marble contrasting with the whitish stone. In the choir (7) there is a good set of fourteenth-century misericords, a remarkable stone pulpit and, in the centre, King John's tomb (8). The marble top dates from about the time of his death, 1216. St George's Chapel (9) displays the colours of the Worcestershire Regiment and military memorials, including one to 'Woodbine Willie' (Studdert Kennedy). Beside the high altar is the exquisite chantry chapel (10) of the elder son of Henry VII, Prince Arthur, who died at Ludlow in 1502, aged fifteen, leaving his brother to inherit the throne as Henry VIII. The entrance to the crypt is in the south transept (11). For over nine hundred years pilgrims have visited this simple holy place. Originally there were 120 pillars, a forest of stone; the idea of a cluster of arches all from one pillar (at the altar end) was copied in the chapter house. The wall lights feature the St Wulstan Cross. Through the Prior's

Door (12), outside to the south, lie the lovely fifteenth-century cloisters (13); the bosses of the south range (14) represent the Tree of Jesse. The windows in the cloisters constitute a unique pageant of the history of the Christian Church in England. The Norman chapter house (15) was the first to be vaulted from a central pillar. The celebrated Three Choirs Festival alternates between Worcester, Gloucester and Hereford. The strains of music across the Severn are unforgettable.

The Music and Light Appeal was launched in 2004 as part of the cathedral's Development and Restoration Trust. Conservation and preservation, too, are always in the minds of cathedral custodians; this is true in the library here, where visitors may see ancient manuscripts and music manuscripts of Edward Elgar and Thomas Tomkins. In 2015 a new Magna Carta Anthem was sung here and at other cathedrals and churches associated with King John, to commemorate that tremendously important historic document. The 'Guild of Benefactors', which is open to all, helps to ensure the future of the building, its mission and ministry.

King John rests in peace between two saints, Oswald and Wulstan.

YORK
CATHEDRAL CHURCH OF ST PETER

Diocese: part of North Yorkshire, the East Riding, a tiny part of West Yorkshire. Founded as a cathedral early in the seventh century, c.627. The Mother Church of the Northern Province.

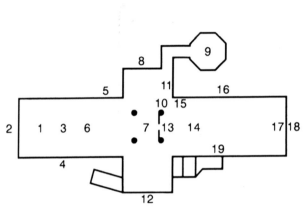

1. Nave
2. Great West Window
3. Roof bosses
4. Jesse Window
5. Bellfounder's Window
6. Dragon's head
7. Lantern tower
8. Five Sisters Window
9. Chapter house
10. Clock
11. Astronomical clock
12. South transept
13. Fifteenth-century screen
14. Choir
15. Tomb of Prince William
16. Window to St William of York
17. Lady Chapel
18. East Window
19. Crypt

THIS CATHEDRAL, FAMILIARLY known as York Minster, is built on the site of the Roman headquarters in Eboracum, where Constantine I was proclaimed Emperor of Rome in 306. He was the first emperor to be converted to Christianity. A minster is primarily a centre for mission. On Easter Day 627, in a little wooden church built for the purpose, the Saxon King Edwin was baptised by Paulinus, the first Archbishop of York, 'with all the nobility and a large number of humbler folk'. From such humble beginnings grew Britain's largest medieval cathedral. The present building is massive, conveying a unique feeling of spaciousness. However, there are small treasures, not least an ancient piece of stained glass (*c.*1150) in the north-west of the nave.

The nave (1) is in the Decorated Gothic style and is one of the widest in Europe; but unfortunately only the side aisles are vaulted in stone because the main span was too wide. The Great West Window (2) dates from 1338; it is also known as the 'Heart of Yorkshire' because of the shape of the central tracery (see page 32). The quantity of medieval stained glass here and elsewhere in the cathedral is exceptional; there is more than in any other English church. Roof bosses (3) in the nave depict the life of Christ and his mother. Notice the Jesse Window (4) and the Bellfounder's Window (5). The curious dragon's head (6) is the pivot of a crane, perhaps to raise a font cover. The lantern tower (7) between the thirteenth-century transepts was rebuilt in the fifteenth century. The famous Five Sisters Window (8) is the largest and finest medieval grisaille window in the world. In the north transept there are two clocks; one strikes the hours and

Among York Minster's treasure of glorious stained glass, the Jesse Window represents the family tree of Jesus. His ancestor, Jesse, is at the bottom; above him is King David, then Solomon, the Virgin Mary, and Jesus himself at the top. Other ancestors appear elsewhere in the window, which dates from about 1310.

The three great towers of York Minster rise majestically above the city. The central one, the lantern, replaced a bell tower that collapsed in 1407 (note the absence of pinnacles).

Opposite: The nave of York Minster is one of the finest of the Decorated period (1291–1340s) and at 93ft in height, is second only to Westminster Abbey. Only the side aisles could be vaulted in stone, however, while the central nave ceiling is, surprisingly, of wood.

quarters (10) and the other is an astronomical clock (11). From this transept one reaches the very beautiful late-thirteenth-century Decorated chapter house (9), with its high wooden vault ingeniously suspended from a domed roof. The south transept (12) was miraculously and expertly restored after a fire in 1984, including the rose window. The niches of the impressively large, late-fifteenth-century screen (13) contain statues of kings from William I to Henry VI; in the stone vault of the archway entrance, with its elegant wrought-iron gates, is a superb boss of the Assumption. The choir (14) is mainly Perpendicular in style and one of Britain's chief glories of the period. In the north choir aisle is the only royal tomb in the cathedral, that of Prince William, the ten-year-old son of Edward III (15). A window in this aisle commemorates the life of St William of York (died 1154), whose tomb was much visited by pilgrims (16). The Minster has many other memorials. At the far east end is the Lady Chapel (17), above which glows the huge east window (18), the largest of its kind still complete with its brilliant glass. In St Stephen's Chapel on the north side, the skilful workmanship of the broderers can be seen in the embroidered kneelers; flowers from all over the world are depicted. Among the sturdy pillars of the crypt (19), several of which are carved, and at the head of an old

York Minster: the Doom Stone, a twelfth-century carved stone showing wicked souls being drawn into hell by devils. It was, perhaps, a slab from the west front of the Norman church. It was found in the Deanery garden and was part of a much larger scene.

well, is the Minster font, beautifully topped with a cover by Ninian Comper commemorating the baptism of King Edwin in the Saxon cathedral in 627. A small chapel is set aside as the shrine of St William. Among other relics are the twelfth-century Doom Stone, depicting figures in torment, and the Romanesque York Virgin or Madonna and Child. Together with Chester, Coventry, Lincoln and Wakefield, the York Cycle of Mystery Plays are often revived.

'The history of York is the history of England', said King George VI. York Minster is a good example of a 'national shrine', a cathedral where repair and maintenance have been much highlighted in recent years. In such buildings restoration and daily maintenance costs are enormous. The burden always falls on the deans and chapters so appeals and sometimes admission charges are, it seems, inevitable. John Sentamu, a High Court Judge in Uganda, was enthroned the 97th Archbishop of York here, 30th November 2005. The ceremony involved the Archbishop playing drums amidst African singing and dancing. He is often in the news for his appeal for justice and peace both at home and abroad. His fasts and 'Vigils of Hope and Trust for World Peace and Reconciliation' held in the Minster are a challenge to all. Other challenges are being met through enterprises and initiatives such as 'York Minster Revealed, Stoneyard and York Glaziers Trust', including the mammoth task of the conservation of the Great East Window. In the latter project much groundbreaking technology is being employed.

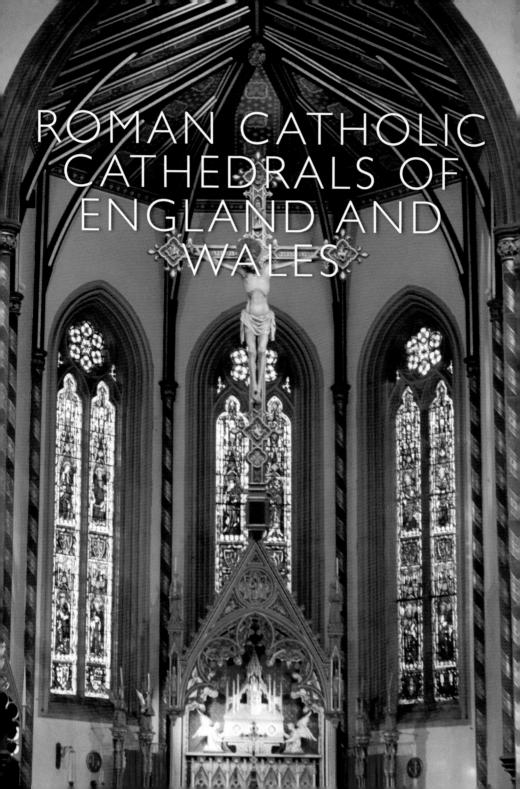

ROMAN CATHOLIC
CATHEDRALS OF
ENGLAND AND
WALES

THE MEDIEVAL CATHEDRALS of England and Wales were built when Roman Catholicism was the established religion. They became Anglican after the Reformation, when the freedom of Roman Catholics to worship according to their faith was first withdrawn and then restricted until the end of the eighteenth century. In 1850 Pope Pius IX restored the Roman Catholic hierarchy in Britain: new dioceses were formed and cathedrals were founded. Most of them were new but some were based on chapels built in the previous fifty years.

Roman Catholic architects engaged on these buildings had a freer hand than architects working on Anglican projects. Augustus Welby Pugin, who was a convert to Roman Catholicism, believed it was the true church and that 'grand and sublime architecture' still had its place. For him, moreover, the Gothic style was the only true style for a cathedral church, and he wrote several books about it. Another bonus for the Roman Catholics (although they had lost a great heritage to the Anglicans, some would argue) was that they were often building on entirely new sites.

ALDERSHOT
CATHEDRAL CHURCH OF ST MICHAEL AND ST GEORGE

This was originally built in the 1890s for the Anglican chaplaincies of the British Army but it was not needed for that purpose so it became the cathedral of the Roman Catholic Bishop to the Armed Forces. The exterior is of red brick and the interior yellow brick with some good stained glass and a beautiful mosaic of the Last Supper. The tall tower with a spire is a prominent landmark.

ARUNDEL
CATHEDRAL CHURCH OF OUR LADY AND ST PHILIP HOWARD (ORIGINALLY NERI)

The cathedral was built in the early 1870s and became the

The grand rose window at Arundel Cathedral.

cathedral of the diocese of Arundel and Brighton in 1965. The architect, J. A. Hansom, working with his son, was provided with adequate finance compared with other architects building cathedrals. He was also well supported by the Dukes of Norfolk, whose seat is at Arundel, and whose family are among Britain's most prominent Roman Catholics. The cathedral is in the Flamboyant style more typical of France (rather like Beauvais Cathedral). There is an impressive rose window and other notable glass.

BIRMINGHAM
CATHEDRAL CHURCH OF ST CHAD

Built as a procathedral in 1839–41, this is one of the earliest and most significant designs of A. W. N. Pugin. It is a large building in mass-produced brick. Tall slender columns and windows emphasise space. There is an apsidal east end and the hillside site allowed for a crypt. There are two small slender spires on either side of the decoratively detailed west end, and some splendid nineteenth-century stained glass. This is an exceptionally fine example of Pugin's work.

BRENTWOOD
CATHEDRAL CHURCH OF ST MARY AND ST HELEN

This is one of England's newest cathedrals. A new parish church was built here in Gothic style in 1861; it became a cathedral in 1917. Around the sanctuary and choir of that church Quinlan Terry built a cathedral in the classical style; this building was dedicated in 1991. Appropriately, the semicircular portico was inspired by one at St Paul's and the octagonal cupola is in the Bernini-Wren style. Inside it is light and spacious, lit by day by large windows of hand-made glass and by night by chandeliers such as might be found in a Wren church. It is beautifully appointed, with Tuscan columns along the nave and supporting the altar. Above the arches are the terracotta roundels depicting Stations of the Cross by Raphael Maklouf and over the altar is an octagonal lantern. Beyond, the 1861 church is incorporated to form the choir and, to the north in the old sanctuary, the Chapel of the Blessed Sacrament.

CARDIFF
CATHEDRAL CHURCH OF ST DAVID

The church was built in 1884–7 to a design of Peter Paul Pugin and became a cathedral in 1916. It was badly damaged by a bomb in 1941 but it has been restored. The nave is exceptionally wide.

CLIFTON (BRISTOL)

CATHEDRAL CHURCH OF ST PETER AND ST PAUL

This church replaced the old nineteenth-century cathedral. It was built in only three years from 1970 to 1973, when it was consecrated in June; it was dubbed the 'ecclesiastical bargain of the century'. The design is imaginative, based on a hexagon and equilateral triangles. There is day lighting from the roof, not windows; the mysterious, evocative interior has many unconventional features such as a Portland stone font in a pool of water and low-relief sculptures of 'The Way of the Cross'.

LANCASTER

CATHEDRAL CHURCH OF ST PETER

Built in 1859 to a design by E. J. Paley, it became a cathedral in 1924. The style is of the Middle Ages, c.1300, and one of Paley's grandest and finest works. The imposing tower and spire, 240 feet high, are probably the finest in Lancashire. The nave and chancel (which has fine stained glass) are also lofty, culminating in an apse. The wooden vault of the chancel retains its original painting. There was extensive restoration in the mid 1990s, incorporating new furnishings. There is a fine late nineteenth-century 'Te Deum' window – We Praise You, O God

LEEDS

CATHEDRAL CHURCH OF ST ANNE

The first Leeds Cathedral was built in the late 1830s, although it did not become a cathedral until 1878. The present building, on a fresh site, is in a kind of Arts and Crafts Gothic by J. H. Eastwood and dates from 1902–4. It has a wide nave and chancel and incorporates some features from the earlier cathedral, such as the Pugin reredos in the south chancel chapel. Changes and refurbishing have taken place from the 1960s onwards, including the Martyr Chapel.

The Bishop's Throne in Brentwood Cathedral, based on a design from a church in Florence, is flanked by elegant Tuscan columns. Several classical elements are represented here: Doric and Ionic pilasters and Palladian windows in this 'restrained' sacred space. Above, however, is a ceiling of richness, its patterns highlighted in gold leaf.

At Clifton, the approach from the west via an atrium or terrace leads to St Paul's Portal (the opposite one is St Peter's). Inside, the narthex has two stunning windows containing eight thousand pieces of glass gathered from all over Europe, representing Pentecost and Jubilation.

LIVERPOOL
METROPOLITAN CATHEDRAL CHURCH OF CHRIST THE KING

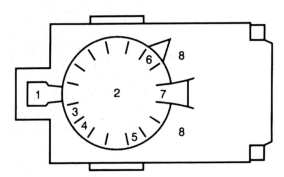

1. Bronze fibreglass doors
2. Central lantern
3. Font
4. Chapel of St George and the English Martyrs
5. Chapel of St Thomas Aquinas
6. Lady Chapel
7. Chapel of the Blessed Sacrament
8. Crypt, Pontifical Hall, St Nicholas Chapel and other amenities

THE ARCHDIOCESE WAS founded in 1850. An earlier cathedral, begun in 1933 to a design by Sir Edwin Lutyens, was eventually abandoned; only the crypt had been built of what was intended to be a huge and ambitious project, over 250,000 square feet and of longitudinal design. Edward Welby Pugin had also envisaged a design, in High Gothic. Sir Frederick Gibberd won the design competition to build the present cathedral. Consecrated in May 1967, it incorporates most ingeniously the earlier crypt (damaged by fire in 1992) but it is circular, of steel and concrete faced with Portland stone, with a central altar and peripheral chapels. It is entered through bronze fibreglass doors (1), which lead into the high porch beneath the bell tower, through a low link into the vast space bathed in multicoloured light from the central lantern (2). This is one great circular window by John Piper and Patrick Reyntiens. Below is the white marble altar on which stands a slender crucifix by Elizabeth Frink. Above is the baldachino of aluminium tubing. There is much twentieth-century artistry and craftsmanship: notice the baptistery with the simple white marble font (3); more windows by Piper and Reyntiens

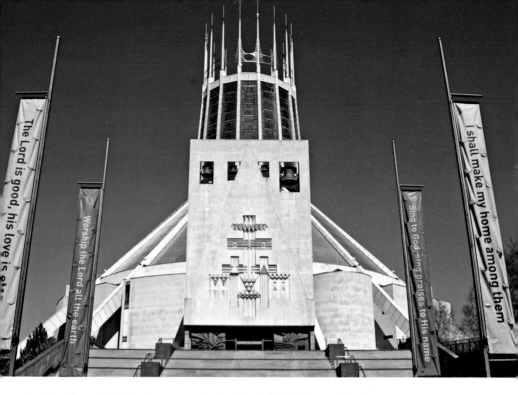

in the Chapel of St George and the English Martyrs (4); the Pentecost mosaic by George Mayer-Martin in the Chapel of St Thomas Aquinas (5), known as the Teachers' Chapel; the matching designs by Ceri Richards for the Chapel of the Blessed Sacrament (7), the largest chapel; the evocative ceramic statue by Robert Brumby of Our Lady and the Child Jesus in the Lady Chapel (6); and in the crypt (8), the huge marble rolling-stone gate to the Pontifical Chapel and the lovely bronze, 'Our Lady of Liverpool', by David John. The brickwork of the crypt is masterly.

Together with the massive Anglican cathedral at the other end of Hope Street, it provides a unique skyline for the great Merseyside city and port; the Unity Chapel testifies to this. In the Amnesty Chapel in the west porch a candle wrapped in barbed wire reminds us of present-day persecution. The Golden Book of Remembrance in its own chapel recalls that 'this Great Cathedral was built by the people of the Archdiocese of Liverpool'.

The Crown of Thorns of Christ the King: endearingly dubbed 'Paddy's Wigwam', the 290 foot lantern dome sits crown-like above Liverpool Metropolitan Cathedral's sanctuary. Here the altar, the focal point, is a block of white marble from near Skopje in Macedonia.

MIDDLESBROUGH

CATHEDRAL CHURCH OF ST MARY

The diocese was founded in 1878. The old cathedral was in the town centre. This new cathedral, begun in 1985, is built in the new satellite town of Coulby Newham about 5 miles to the south. The new building embodies the very best in modern craftsmanship; 'to create a building in total accord with the principles underlying new forms of worship'. Basically the design is a semicircular plan with multi-purpose areas; there are also a Blessed Sacrament Chapel, a social hall, offices and so on. The cathedral's special symbol, its logo, is the Steps to Heaven Cross representing suffering and resurrection; it was designed by a group of schoolboys. The cross surmounts the roof and there is a distinctive campanile housing three nineteenth-century bells.

NEWCASTLE UPON TYNE

CATHEDRAL CHURCH OF ST MARY

Begun in 1841 and completed, but for the tower and spire, in 1844, this cathedral was designed by A.W. N. Pugin with a nave with separately roofed aisles. On the south-west tower (by J. A. Hansom, 1860), over the modern entrance porch, is a needle spire with spirelets. There is stained glass from the nineteenth and twentieth centuries and a frieze of inscribed tiles. The exterior is very impressive.

NORTHAMPTON

CATHEDRAL CHURCH OF OUR LADY AND ST THOMAS OF CANTERBURY

The church here became a cathedral in 1850. A. W. N. Pugin built the small church of St Felix, with low arcades and a tall clerestory, in 1844. It became part of the sacristy of the greatly enlarged cathedral built from 1862 to 1864 and designed by his son, who added a nave, aisles and a western apse; the eastern part of the church dates from 1948–60. The west

The Cathedral Church of Our Lady and St Thomas of Canterbury, Northampton has a fine, sturdy tower at the crossing.

tower was never built, but there is a crossing tower. Stained glass windows represent saints with local associations.

NORWICH

CATHEDRAL CHURCH OF ST JOHN BAPTIST

This handsome church (set on very high ground, level with the base of the Anglican cathedral's spire) became a cathedral in 1976. The Roman Catholic Dukes of Norfolk (see Arundel) were generous benefactors. It was built between 1882 and 1910 to the design of George Gilbert Scott and completed by his brother. Always of cathedral size, it is a beautiful and impressive church in the Early English Gothic style, with massive cylindrical columns and finely carved capitals; richly moulded arches support a triforium of clustered pillars. At the end of the long nave rises the splendid painted and gilded calvary by Peter Rendle. There are fine details of decoration and furnishing throughout and some good stained glass by the Powells, father and son. Note especially the Walsingham Chapel.

NOTTINGHAM

CATHEDRAL CHURCH OF ST BARNABAS

A cathedral since 1850, the church was built in the Early English style in the 1840s to A. W. N. Pugin's design: a cruciform building in the Early English style with octagonal piers and double chamfered arches with an imposing crossing steeple. Unfortunately, few of the original furnishings remain; examples are the Crucifix and some of Pugin's stained glass.

PLYMOUTH

CATHEDRAL CHURCH OF ST MARY AND ST BONIFACE

A cathedral since 1858, it was designed by J. A. Hansom in the Early English Gothic style with a 200 foot spire. There is a large hanging crucifix.

PORTSMOUTH

CATHEDRAL CHURCH OF ST JOHN THE EVANGELIST

Designed by John Crawley and later by J. A. Hansom, this church became a cathedral in 1882 and was built in the 1880s and 1890s in dark brick in the Decorated Gothic style. Much repair work was done after Second World War bomb damage. There is some good modern stained glass. The internal arrangement has been adjusted five times, the last occasion being in 1982, a century after the foundation of the diocese.

SALFORD

CATHEDRAL CHURCH OF ST JOHN THE EVANGELIST

A cathedral since 1850, the church was built in the 1840s. A. W. N. Pugin's original design was not used; instead Matthew Hadfield based his design on three medieval churches, Howden, Newark and Selby, and built a cruciform church in yellow-grey stone with a central tower and spire. There was some rearrangement in the early 1970s, including a new sanctuary at the crossing. There is a valued ministry to the homeless.

SHEFFIELD
CATHEDRAL CHURCH OF ST MARIE

A cathedral since 1980, the church stands on the site of a mission in an area laid out for the Dukes of Norfolk in the eighteenth century (see Arundel and Norwich). It was built in the 1840s to a design by Matthew Hadfield based on fourteenth-century Geometrical and Decorated styles.

The lofty spacious interior of the Cathedral Church of St John the Evangelist, Portsmouth.

There is a majestic south-west tower with a spire with three tiers of dormers. It was considered by some to be the finest Roman Catholic church in the style, at least up to the mid 1970s, when much of note was removed during the reordering. There is the tomb of the founder, the Reverend Charles Pratt.

SHREWSBURY
CATHEDRAL CHURCH OF OUR LADY HELP OF CHRISTIANS AND ST PETER OF ALCANTARA

A cathedral since 1850, the church is in a pleasant setting and was one of the first of the 'new' cathedrals envisaged by A. W. N. Pugin, but he died before building started in 1853 to a further design by his son, a grander project than what was actually built. The nave is lofty with slender pillars and elaborately carved capitals. Even without a tower it is an impressive church. The stained glass windows by Margaret Rope are outstanding.

SOUTHWARK
CATHEDRAL CHURCH OF ST GEORGE

A cathedral since 1850, the church was built in 1840–8 to A. W. N. Pugin's design, which had to be revised and was never completely fulfilled. In 1850 it was the first Roman Catholic cathedral in England since the Reformation. It was almost entirely destroyed in the London Blitz and only a vestige of Pugin's aspirations remains. Some reordering took place in 1989. There is a lofty nave of Cotswold stone, affording a bright and spacious interior.

SWANSEA
CATHEDRAL CHURCH OF ST JOSEPH

Designed by the younger Pugin in the Gothic style and built in a very depressed area, it remains a symbol of the people's great faith. It became a cathedral in 1987 when the new diocese of Menevia was formed (reverting to the old see of St David's).

WESTMINSTER

CATHEDRAL CHURCH OF THE MOST PRECIOUS HOLY BLOOD, ST MARY, ST JOSEPH AND ST PETER

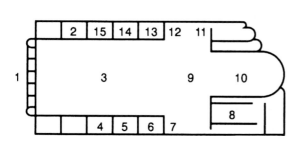

1. West front
2. Campanile
3. Nave
4. Chapel of St Patrick and the Irish Saints
5. Chapel of St Andrew
6. Chapel of St Paul
7. Figure of the Virgin Mary
8. Lady Chapel
9. Crucifix
10. Sanctuary with dome above
11. Blessed Sacrament Chapel
12. Chapel of St Thomas of Canterbury
13. Chapel of St Joseph
14. Chapel of St George
15. Chapel of Holy Souls

THE ARCHITECT, John Francis Bentley, a convert to Roman Catholicism, was commissioned in 1894 although he had never before created a major building; moreover, compared with architects of Anglican projects, he had a much freer hand. This splendid cathedral, one of London's great monuments, is Byzantine in inspiration, very un-English, with abundant marble and mosaic throughout. The west front (1) is of red brick (twelve million bricks were used in construction) with contrasting horizontal bands of white Portland stone. A 284 foot Italian-style campanile (2) rises in the north-west corner.

Inside, the cathedral is elaborately impressive. Three great vaulted domed bays supported by massive piers form the nave (3), and beyond the magnificent great crucifix (9), suspended from the main arch, can be seen the dome of the sanctuary (10) above a circle of windows lighting the marble baldachino over the altar. Fourteen panels sculpted by Eric Gill depict the stations of the cross. Chapels open from the nave aisles, fitted and adorned with the finest materials and craftsmanship. In the south-west (right) corner is the Baptistery, then the Chapel of St Gregory and St Augustine; the tomb of Cardinal Archbishop Basil Hume OM (1923–99) is here. Fine Irish marbles and the

The broad piazza welcomes and enables one to appreciate, on approach, the striking Italianate exterior of Westminster Cathedral, of brick banded with white Portland stone – an oasis of peace in busy central London.

shamrock decorate the Chapel of St Patrick and the Irish Saints (4), while the Chapel of St Andrew (5) is the most Byzantine in the cathedral, with fine mosaics, but also with splendid inlaid ebony choir stalls by Ernest Gimson. Over the Chapel of St Paul (6) spreads a tent-like mosaic canopy recalling Paul's trade as a tent-maker. Across the broad south transept is the sumptuous Lady Chapel (8); to the left before it is a lovely medieval English alabaster figure of the Virgin Mary (7). In the sanctuary (10) the massive marble altar is magnificent below the superb baldachino. Look for fine mosaics of a peacock and of a phoenix by Boris Anrep at the entrance to the Blessed Sacrament Chapel (11). Dramatic columns of black and white marble feature in the Chapel of St Thomas of Canterbury (12) in the north transept, also known as the Vaughan Chantry, where the founder is commemorated. Next are the Chapel of St Joseph (13) and

The grand Byzantine interior of Westminster Cathedral.

the Chapel of St George (14), with the shrine of St John Southworth. Nearby, Alban, Britain's first Christian martyr, is commemorated in a mosaic (2001) by Christopher Webb. The Chapel of Holy Souls (15), was designed by Bentley but not decorated in his lifetime. The semicircular vaulted crypt is below the sanctuary. Also below and reached from the Baptistery at the west end there are various amenities, including the Cathedral Kitchen restaurant. This cathedral should not be confused with Westminster Abbey up the road, an Anglican national shrine of cathedral proportions but which is not a cathedral church and thus not within the remit of this book. This foremost Roman Catholic cathedral has a wide-reaching and diverse ministry, ranging from The Passage (for day and night care of the homeless) to an American Friends link.

WREXHAM
CATHEDRAL CHURCH OF OUR LADY OF SORROWS

The parish church built in 1857 to a design by Edward Pugin, son of A. W. N. Pugin, in 1907 became the procathedral of the diocese of Menevia. In February 1987 it became the cathedral church of the newly formed diocese of Wrexham (see also under Swansea). The style is Decorated Gothic of the Middle Ages but the whole effect is restrained and homely to suit a parish church. In keeping with ancient Christian custom, the bishop's throne is central, beneath the east window (compare Norwich Anglican Cathedral). There are various memorial windows, a fine replica of Michelangelo's *Pieta* and also an icon of Mary, a gift of the local Polish community. As part of the cathedral's work to mark the Millennium, there is an icon to commemorate the local martyr Richard Gwyn, executed on 15th October 1584.

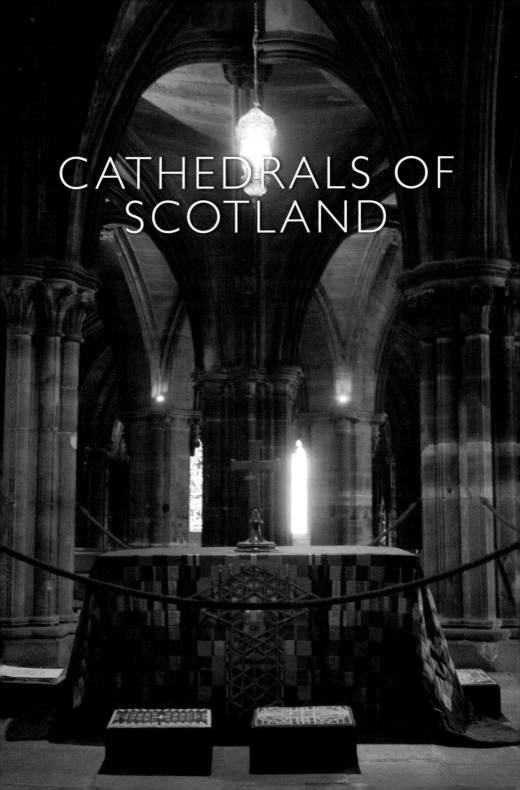

CATHEDRALS OF SCOTLAND

Previous page:
The tomb of
St Mungo in the
crypt at Glasgow
Cathedral.

The breathtaking
ruins of the
thirteenth-
century west
end of Elgin
Cathedral (see
page 254).

THE EARLIEST CATHEDRAL in Scotland and in the British Isles was at Whithorn in Galloway – *Candida Casa* or the 'white house' founded by Ninian in 397. Lismore, an island at the mouth of Loch Linnhe, was the site of the cathedral of the Bishops of Argyll until they moved to Iona in 1507.

The reformed or protestant faith became established in Scotland from 1560, largely in the form of Presbyterianism. This suited Elizabeth I of England, for Presbyterians were also opposed to Mary, Queen of Scots. Mary's son, James VI (James I of England), contented himself with being allowed to appoint bishops but Charles I precipitated the Civil War by insisting on Anglican worship as well. Presbyterianism was re-established. Charles II went back on his word to the Scots and reimposed the episcopacy. After years of bitter strife Scotland finally got rid of bishops under William and Mary in 1690, from which time the Church of Scotland has been Presbyterian. Consequently the ancient cathedrals lost their function. A few are glorious ruins, wholly or in part (for example, Dunblane, Dunkeld and Elgin). The rest are no longer cathedrals in the official episcopal sense, that is, the seats of bishops. Consequently these ancient buildings, although architecturally and historically most interesting, do not strictly come within the scope of this book.

CATHEDRALS OF FORMER TIMES

ABERDEEN

St Machar's, founded 1150. Nothing remains. The later church, too, has lost its crossing, transepts and choir. The two impressive features are the west front with two fortified towers, each with a low spire, and the wooden ceiling of the nave, with many heraldic shields. Red sandstone has been used at the east end and there is some good carving. Later building was in granite, which appears somewhat austere.

BIRNIE

Late twelfth century. The bishopric of Moray was founded by Alexander I in 1107 and the first cathedral church was here. It was moved later to Spynie (1203) and then Elgin. Birnie Kirk is a small building, plain but beautifully constructed.

BRECHIN

Founded in the mid twelfth century by David I on the site of an abbey. There are two asymmetrical towers at the west end, including the impressive and rare round tower of *c.*1000, 87 feet high, originally set apart and later incorporated into the cathedral.

DORNOCH

Founded in 1224. It was largely rebuilt in the nineteenth century by the Duchess of Sutherland. Most of it was destroyed by fire in 1570. It is the burial place of sixteen Earls of Sutherland. Note the Andrew Carnegie memorial.

The finest of the four remaining crown steeples in Scotland graces Edinburgh's Cathedral Church of St Giles, rising proudly over the Royal Mile and the city. This fine building is steeped in the history of Scotland. St Giles, born in Athens in 640, lived later in France, Scotland's oldest ally – hence the honour of being Edinburgh's patron saint.

DUNBLANE

Founded in the mid twelfth century, it was roofless for three hundred years after the Reformation and restored 1889–93; a heavily restored church remains. St Blane built a church here in the sixth century. The thirteenth-century west door and the six rare, elaborately carved stalls with canopies and misericords are of note. John Ruskin, art patron and critic in the Victorian era held the place in high esteem, considering its arches and windows impressive.

DUNKELD

An abbey in 815, a cathedral in 1120. The choir is used as a church. The ruined nave and north-west tower are impressive.

EDINBURGH

St Giles. It was built in the late fourteenth and early fifteenth centuries. The tower has a conspicuous crown, a famous landmark on the Royal Mile and on the skyline of Scotland's capital. At the Reformation it was divided into several 'churches'. The Thistle Chapel dates from 1911. It is a great church with many historical associations, not least with the Protestant reformer John Knox.

ELGIN

Founded 1224. Called the 'Lantern of the North', it is a splendid ruin of some of the finest early Gothic building in Scotland. Do not miss the chapter house with its central pier and vaulting. The keeper of

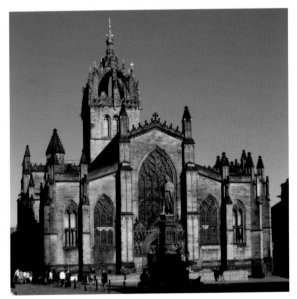

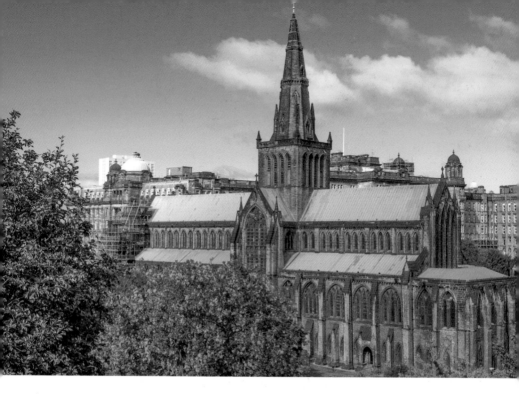

the ruins, John Shanks, appointed in 1825, is said to have cleared the accumulated rubble single-handedly (picture on page 252).

FORTROSE

On the Black Isle, this was the see of the former Bishops of Ross. Cromwell's men used this medieval building as a quarry for the fort at Inverness. Little remains but the ruins are impressive. What is seen today was built at the instigation of the Countess of Ross Euthema for her burial and chantry. In Shakespeare's *Macbeth*, Forres is the site of King Duncan's court.

GLASGOW

St Mungo or St Kentigern, founded in 1123. The most complete medieval church in Scotland to survive intact has a 225 foot high spire on the thirteenth-century tower and an impressive, intriguing crypt with an eastern ambulatory and four chapels – the 'Laigh Kirk' – which is the site of St Mungo's tomb; he died

Christians have worshipped on the site of St Mungo's cathedral in Glasgow for 1500 years. St Ninian, an early missionary, was buried here in AD 397, two hundred years before Augustine evangelised southern Britain. This present church is the fourth on the site and it is the finest early Gothic church in Scotland.

in 603. The cathedral possesses some fine twentieth-century stained glass. The fifteenth-century screen is now unique in Scotland and there is some rare wall painting.

IONA

St Mary, founded in 563 by St Columba. For four hundred years this remote island was the centre of Celtic Christianity and the burial place of early Scottish kings. This cathedral dates mainly from the late fifteenth and sixteenth centuries. It became a cathedral when the Bishop moved here from Lismore. It was wonderfully restored in the twentieth century with the establishment of the world-famous Iona Community under the able and inspired leadership of the late Reverend George MacLeod. The cathedral with its 70 foot tower and the ancient Celtic crosses before the west front is an unforgettable sight. The aisle-less nave and the whole place evoke an impression of prayerfulness, serenity and rugged simplicity. The pier and half arch of the south choir aisle are unusual. John Smith, leader of the Labour Party, who died in May 1994, is buried in the churchyard.

A place of pilgrimage and spiritual renewal on a lonely Hebridean island off the west coast of Scotland, Iona Cathedral is world-renowned and has been for centuries, from the time of St Columba in the sixth century right up to the present. It is now the home of the Iona ecumenical community.

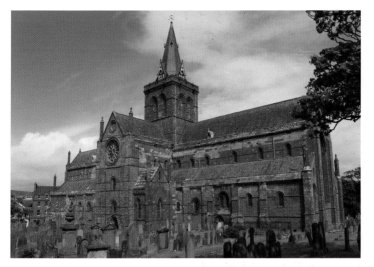

The splendid Norman Romanesque Cathedral of St Magnus, Kirkwall, with traces of later Gothic architecture. Magnus was adopted as the Patron Saint of the Orkney Islands. This is the most northerly cathedral in the United Kingdom.

KIRKWALL (ORKNEY)

St Magnus, founded in 1137 by Rognvald Jarl III (under Norwegian archiepiscopal care until 1472). The splendid Norman Romanesque red sandstone church became ruinous but was restored in the early twentieth century. The west front has early Gothic doorways. Through a royal charter granted in 1486, it belongs to the local community and not to any specific denomination or church. Close by is notable Renaissance architecture.

ST ANDREWS

Possibly founded in the eighth century. It became a bishopric in 908 and the cathedral was begun in 1160. It was Scotland's largest cathedral. Badly damaged at the Reformation, it is now almost completely ruined. From St Regulus Tower there are fine views over this ancient university town and the coastal area with its famous golf course.

SPYNIE

Was the cathedral of Moray from the early thirteenth century; it was destroyed in 1736.

CATHEDRALS OF THE SCOTTISH EPISCOPAL CHURCH

THESE ARE ALL nineteenth-century buildings. There are seven dioceses in full communion with, but independent of, the Church of England.

ABERDEEN

Cathedral Church of St Andrew (cathedral 1914). Diocese of Aberdeen and Orkney/Shetland. This is an early Gothic Revival church in the Perpendicular style designed by the locally born architect Archibald Simpson (1817). The chancel is by G. E. Street and dates from 1880. There is a memorial to the consecration in 1784 of the first Bishop of the American Episcopal Church and of the Anglican Communion outside the British Isles. Coats of arms of forty-eight of the states of the USA are in the vaulted side aisles. Restoration from 1934 to 1943 was by Sir John Ninian Comper. This cathedral is fully involved in the contemporary world of inner-city Aberdeen, as a glance at a list of activities and concerns will show.

DUNDEE

Cathedral Church of St Paul (for the diocese of Brechin). Designed by Sir George Gilbert Scott (1852–5), it is in the Decorated Gothic style, including the 220 foot spire. There is an elaborate memorial effigy of Alexander Penrose Forbes, the first Bishop.

EDINBURGH

Cathedral Church of St Mary. This vast, beautiful church is among the finest of the nineteenth-century Gothic Revival cathedrals. Designed by Sir George Gilbert Scott, it was consecrated in 1879, a year after his death. Various architectural features refer to Gothic work in Scotland; for example the triforium of the nave recalls Dunblane. Four buttresses carry an octagon that rises into pinnacles and the central spire soars to 330 feet. There are two spires on the west front, which is graced with all the elements of Gothic architecture. It is also worth noting the stained glass, especially the Te Deum east window and the west window of four lancets and a rose, the three hundred kneelers embroidered by the congregation, the King Charles Chapel (he founded the Diocese of Edinburgh), the Resurrection Chapel, the Hanging Rood and a rare pelican lectern. Here is a prominent welcoming church with many amenities and ministries worthy of Scotland's capital.

At St Mary's, Edinburgh, the central spire rises on four lofty buttresses to an octagon, belfry and pinnacles. One can compare these spires with the 'Ladies of the Vale' at Lichfield, the latter being graceful, those at Edinburgh showing strength and vigour.

GLASGOW

Cathedral Church of St Mary. The diocese stretches down to Galloway and was founded in 1908. This is another great work of Sir George Gilbert Scott, completed in 1870–1. The 205 foot spire was added in 1892–3. The medieval cathedral of St Mungo was the former cathedral. Much restoration work has been undertaken; a new entrance dates from 2002. The murals by Gwyneth Leech are very fine. There are many activities in which the cathedral congregation is involved in the community.

INVERNESS

Cathedral Church of St Andrew. The diocese covers Moray, Ross and Caithness. A memorial commemorates Bishop Robert Eden (from Essex), through whose vision in 1851 this cathedral was built, to the design of a local architect, Alexander Ross, at a basic cost for the structure alone of £15,106 (plus four pence, three farthings!) and consecrated in 1874. It was the first to be built after the Reformation and there is much excellent craftsmanship, especially in the woodwork. Five gold icons were given to the founder in 1861. There is polished granite in the nave and the font is a copy of the famous angel font in Copenhagen Cathedral, Denmark. Stained glass windows portray the life of Jesus. There is an apsidal sanctuary at the east end with three windows, while at the west end the window is one of the largest in Scotland. Here is a welcoming ministry enhanced by the memorable and pleasant siting by the River Ness.

MILLPORT

Cathedral of the Isles and the Collegiate Church of the Holy Spirit. This church was built in the mid nineteenth century on Great Cumbrae Island. St John the Divine in Oban (also nineteenth-century) is the co-cathedral. From 1975 to 1985 the college buildings housed the Community of Celebration from the United States. It is a popular retreat centre. The cathedral is a small building (the smallest cathedral church in the United Kingdom). Designed by William Butterfield, it evokes, however, a feeling of awe and simple sacred beauty. There is much decoration and the ceiling depicts flowers of the islands. Millport Cathedral is a superb spiritual and cultural centre, ideally situated near the sea, with a focus on ministry, both ecumenical and worldwide. As for the co-cathedral in Oban, dating from 1864, a crossing and lantern were added in 1958, followed by more recent restoration.

PERTH

Cathedral Church of St Ninian. Diocese of St Andrews, Dunkeld and Dunblane. This church was built between 1850 and 1890 in the grounds of the old Black Friars monastery, to a conventional design by William Butterfield; some later work is by F. L. Pearson. A lofty building – the nave is 70 feet high – it has attractive stained glass in the nave and in the east and west windows. The rood (Christ Crucified) by Comper contrasts with the statue of the Risen Lord in the Resurrection Chapel at the west end. The baldachino over the high altar is of Cornish granite.

ROMAN CATHOLIC CATHEDRALS

THERE ARE TWO provinces, that of St Andrews and Edinburgh, and that of Glasgow.

ABERDEEN

Cathedral Church of St Mary of the Assumption. Built 1860–80, it has a spire 200 feet high. The diocese is the largest in Scotland. In the 1960s this was the first cathedral church in the British Isles to anticipate liturgical reform. Note the font in a prominent central position, low reliefs (by Ann Davidson) in the nave arch spandrels and Gabriel Loire's mosaics of the Stations of the Cross.

AYR

Cathedral Church of the Good Shepherd (1957). This is a unique dedication for a cathedral church in Britain. The diocese covers Galloway. Until a fire destroyed it in May 1961, St Andrew's church in Dumfries was the procathedral; the cathedral was then moved to Ayr. It could be argued that the Diocese of Galloway is the first historically in the British Isles since Ninian evangelised here in the late fourth century.

DUNDEE

Cathedral Church of St Andrew. There was an earlier church of 1782. The present building dates from the 1830s. This is the diocese of Dunkeld.

EDINBURGH

Cathedral Church of St Mary. Designed by Gillespie Graham, it dates from 1814 and 1890. This is the archbishopric of

St Andrews and Edinburgh. In the 1970s structural changes revealed more of the the façade and the cathedral was rededicated in 1978. Note the 'Coronation of the Virgin' painting by the Belgian Louis Beyart over the sanctuary arch, the memorial stone in the aisle, the 'St Anthony and Christ Child' plaque, the Pieta and the 'Lazarus' painting in the porch. The opening of the annual Edinburgh International Festival is marked with Mass; there is also Mass for the legal profession.

GLASGOW

Metropolitan Cathedral Church of St Andrew. An earlier church dated from the 1790s; the present one from 1814 and also from the late 1880s. The chair or 'cathedra' of the Archbishop is here.

MOTHERWELL

Cathedral Church of Our Lady of Good Aid. It dates from the 1870s but became a cathedral only in 1947. Motherwell takes its name from 'the well of Our Lady'.

OBAN

Cathedral Church of St Columba. This dates from the 1870s and also the 1930s, when the architect was Giles Gilbert Scott. The diocese covers Argyll and the Isles. Sadly this cathedral is not well known. Granite is able to resist the severe coastal wind and weather. The building has a feeling of rugged and lofty simplicity with the altar as a colourful focal point. St John the Divine is the other cathedral church in Oban (Scottish Episcopal).

PAISLEY

Cathedral Church of St Mirin. It was built in the early nineteenth century and in 1932. The town grew up around a Cluniac abbey founded in the twelfth century. St Mirin's shrine was there. An earlier building was the first stone-built Roman Catholic church in post-Reformation Scotland.

FURTHER READING

Adams, Henry. *Mont St Michel and Chartres*. Riverside
    Press, 1963.
Anderson, William, and Hicks, Clive. *Cathedrals in Britain
    and Ireland*. Macdonald & Janes, 1978.

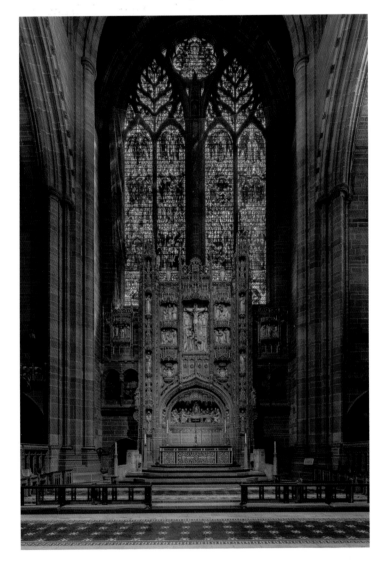

The high altar and reredos, an integral part of the great east wall of Liverpool's Anglican cathedral. In this part of the striking design, the Last Supper is appropriately and movingly represented, reminding all of the saving work of Christ.

Banister, Fletcher. *A History of Architecture*. Architectural Press, 1975.

Camille, Michael. *Gothic Art*. Weidenfeld & Nicolson, 1996.

Cannon, Jon. *Cathedrals – and the world that made them*. Constable, 2011.

Cannon, John. *Medieval Church Architecture*. Shire, 2014.

Clifton-Taylor, Alec. *The Cathedrals of England*. Thames & Hudson, revised edition 1986.

Cormack, Patrick. *English Cathedrals*. Harmony Books, New York, 1984.

Cowan, Painton. *English Stained Glass*. Thames & Hudson, 2008.

Cowan, Painton. *Rose Windows*. Thames & Hudson, 1979 and 2005.

Edwards, David L. *The Cathedrals of Britain*. Pitkin, 1989.

Erlande-Brandenburg, Alain. *The Cathedral Builders of the Middle Ages*. Thames and Hudson, 1995.

Fry, Plantagenet Somerset. *Great Cathedrals*. Windward, 1982.

Harvey, John. *British Cathedrals*. André Deutsch, 1992.

Johnson, Paul. *Cathedrals of England, Scotland and Wales*. Batsford and Weidenfeld & Nicolson, 1993.

Macaulay, David. *Cathedral: The Story of Its Construction*. Atlantic Books, 1981.

Morris, Richard. *Cathedrals and Abbeys of England and Wales*. Dent, 1979.

New, Anthony. *A Guide to the Cathedrals of Britain*. Constable, 1981.

Osborne, June, et al. *Stained Glass in England*. Alan Sutton, 1993.

Pevsner, Nikolaus, and Metcalf, P. *The Cathedrals of England*. Penguin Series, 1985.

Platten, Stephen, and Lewis, Christopher (editors). *Flagships of the Spirit*. Darton Longman & Todd, 1998.

Swaan, Wim, with Brooke, Christopher. *The Gothic Cathedral*. Elek, 1969; Omega Books, 1984.

Tatton-Brown, Tim. *The English Cathedral*. New Holland, 2002.

Taylor, Richard. *How to Read a Church*. Ebury Press, Random House, 2003.

Thorold, Herny, and Burton, Peter. *Collins Guide to the Cathedrals, Abbeys and Priories of England and Wales*. Collins, 1986.

Thurlow, Gilbert. *Cathedrals and Abbeys of England*. Jarrold, 1986.

Various authors. *Pilgrim Guide Series – Themes and Devotions*. Canterbury Press, Norwich.

Wilson, Christopher. *The Gothic Cathedral*. Thames & Hudson, 1992.

Wittich, John. *Exploring Cathedrals*. Pryor, 1996.

Guidebooks to individual cathedrals are published independently and also by Jarrold and Pitkin. Shire also has a strong architectural and religious list of titles.

USEFUL CONTACTS

All of these have websites with up-to-date information, addresses, etc.

Association of English Cathedrals
Cathedral Camps – CSV Heritage Camps Volunteers
Cathedrals Plus/Pilgrims' Association
Cathedral Communications Ltd and Historic Building Conservation
Cathedrals' Advisory Committee and Council for the Care of Churches
Central Council of Church Bellringers
Church Care – Cathedral Tourism Association
A Church Near You
Council for Learning outside the classroom
English Heritage

Friends of Cathedral Music
National Association of Flower Arrangement Societies
The Anglican Communion/The Church of England

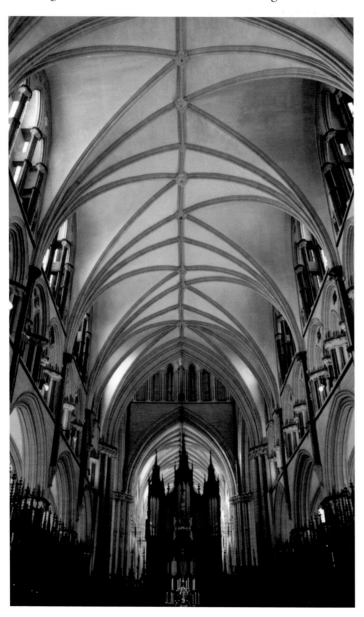

The crazy
asymmetrical
vaulting of
St Hugh's Choir
at Lincoln
(c. 1200). See
pages 133–6.

LOOKING DEEPER (PASTORAL AND LIFESTYLE ISSUES)

Alpha Office, Alpha International
Arthur Rank Centre – The Church and rural issues
Association of Christian Writers
Bible Society. Also Scottish Bible Society
Christian Aid – one of the largest ecumenical charities
Christianity and the Arts
Churches Together in England/Scotland/Wales. All
  denominations have websites – Methodist Church,
  Baptist Union, United Reformed Church, Presbyterian,
  Salvation Army, Society of Friends/the Quakers.
Cursillo (Spanish for 'little course') for spiritual guidance
Embrace – tackling poverty and injustice in the Middle East
Emmaus Correspondence Courses
Fresh Expressions
Greenbelt Festival – the UK's largest Christian art festival
Iona Community – based in the cathedral, ecumenical and
  committed to seeking new ways of living the Gospel
Keswick Ministries – evangelism and mission
New Wine – Local Churches Network – The joy of
  worshipping God
Premier Christian Radio and its various ministries
Rejesus – Story, Lives, Spirituality, Creativity
Retreat Association
Spring Harvest – the largest Christian conference in Europe
Trans World Radio Ltd. – Listening World
United Christian Broadcasters
We Are Us – Anglican Churches working in partnership

PICTURE CREDITS

Most of the pictures in this book were obtained from Flickr, Wikimedia Commons and geograph.co.uk, and were specifically chosen for their free usage licences, not subject to copyright restrictions. Any improper use is accidental and enquiries about this should be addressed to the Publisher. Where full names were not available, user names have been listed. Images are referenced by the pages on which they appear.

INDEX